This map is a representation of the many trading routes (major and minor) that [...] of Silk Road history, many of which are explored further in this book. As such [...] single period. Different routes were of varying importance over time as empires a[...] The place names represent historical names most often used in the Silk Road hist[...] their modern names.

Altay Mountains

Tian Shan

Gulja

Turfan

Hami

Gobi

Kucha

Weili

Aksu

Anxi

Wuyuan

Yangjing

Kashgar

Taklimakan Desert

Loulan

Dunhuang

Hexi Corridor

Yarkand

Miran

Qilian Shan

Niya

Altun Shan

Wuwei

Khotan

Kunlun Shan

Huang

Lanzhou

Chang'an

Luoyang

Yellow Sea

Nancheng

Wancheng

Guangling

Plateau of Tibet

Jiankang

Suzhou

Chendu (Shu)

Yiling

Chang Jiang

Himalaya

Indraprastha

Qianzhong

Changsha

Minzhong

Ganges

ethora

Kanyakubja

Prayaga

Pataliputra

Tamralipta

Panyu

Jiaozhi

Bay of Bengal

South China Sea

NICK ROWAN

THE SILK ROAD
REVISITED

Hertfordshire Press, London 2020

HERTFORDSHIRE PRESS

Hertfordshire Press Ltd © 2020
e-mail: publisher@hertfordshirepress.com
www.hertfordshirepress.com

THE SILK ROAD
REVISITED
BY NICK ROWAN

English

Cover - Registan. Samarkand. View of the Sherdor Madrassah, by Feruz Rustamov

Author's Photo by Xander Casey
Design by Alexandra Rey
Map by Thomas Bachrach
Editing & Additional Research by Paul Robert Walker

*British Library Catalogue in Publication Data
A catalogue record for this book is available from the British Library
Library of Congress in Publication Data
A catalogue record for this book has been requested*

ISBN: 978-1-913356-07-1

CONTENTS

7 AUTHOR'S NOTE
11 ACKNOWLEDGEMENTS

INTRODUCTION
12 THE SILK ROAD TODAY

CHAPTER ONE
26 THE MEDITERRANEAN: VENICE TO CONSTANTINOPLE

CHAPTER TWO
40 GATEWAY TO ASIA: TURKEY

CHAPTER THREE
54 LAND OF EMPIRES: PERSIA

CHAPTER FOUR
70 HEART OF THE SILK ROAD: TURKMENISTAN, UZBEKISTAN, AND TAJIKISTAN

CHAPTER FIVE
92 THE MOUNTAINS AND THE STEPPES: KYRGYZSTAN AND KAZAKHSTAN

CHAPTER SIX
108 THE LAND OF SILK: CHINA

140 TIMELINE OF KEY SILK ROAD HISTORICAL EVENTS
144 SELECTED BIBLIOGRAPHY & FURTHER READING

For Deborah, Olivia & Matilda

The whitewashed halls of the Po-i-Kalyan mosque in Bukhara.

THE SILK ROAD REVISITED

AUTHOR'S NOTE

I have never considered myself a historian nor did I ever intend to write a history of any place or period, but I have, perhaps, become an accidental historian. My inspiration came from my travels over the years to parts of Eastern Europe, the Middle East, Central Asia and China, retracing the route of the old Silk Road. It became a fascinating obsession trying to piece together all the characters, places and events – names I kept hearing but couldn't always quite place.

In my travels, I became aware that although today the idea of the Silk Road is banded around ever more freely by academics and marketing folk alike, few really understood or had been able to put today's "Silk Road" into its historical context. Therefore, this book was born out of a desire to link together as many of the places, religions, people and cultures that one might encounter in the course of everyday life along the Silk Road of today. There are many famous historical events, names from literature and scientific innovations that originated thanks to the Silk Road but which we take for granted today. The text that accompanies the wonderful photographs showcasing today's Silk Road cannot hope to capture anywhere near the full, or even an abridged, version of the Silk Road's splendid history. However, I hope in some small way you will find yourself going, "aha, so that is where that comes from," and perhaps drawing the odd smile as you read and enjoy the rich cultural heritage the Silk Road has left behind for us to marvel at today.

I learned much of my Silk Road history in only the most basic of manners as I travelled from place to place and met the descendants of the Silk Road's past. It was a set of stories, that often felt unrelated or far-fetched, moulded into a vaguely consecutive timeline of events, each with their own heroes and villains. My school history syllabus barely covered the region and what it did cover did little to inspire me towards further adventure and discovery. It greatly missed providing the realisation that the world has ever been thus connected. A realisation that perhaps can only really be made by visiting the relics of time in the countries where they exist. The ancient world was far more interlinked and connected than we are often led to believe. The recent increase in the speed of digital information sharing has transformed our world, but we should never forget that similar transformations were still going on even centuries ago and I feel that should amaze us in at least equal measure.

I have purposefully written the chapters from West to East – as a European perhaps it is my natural instinct to do it this way. It is the direction I took in my own travels as I ventured from the familiar to the unknown.

It is the way of Marco Polo's journey of discovery too. There is no right or wrong way to write about the Silk Road trading routes since they emerged from both ends of the world and met, often messily, in the middle. Indeed, the story of China, and my own chapter, essentially has to fall back to an East to West direction in large parts as that was the flow of the early Silk Road story from that region as it encountered Central Asia and Europe. Since many write the Silk Road's history the other way round, I decided to stick to what has just felt natural to me.

I have also tried not to get too bogged down in transliteration – I have let myself be guided by how different names of people and cities have come out in the resources or local languages that they are referred in. Where a more modern or Western name felt appropriate, I have used that name, but where the mythology or mystique is better captured by a different version, I have used that. I think the book is the better for it but to those who are frustrated by the inconsistency, I ask forgiveness in advance.

The saying goes that travel broadens the mind and it is true. What I find is even truer, however, is that every time you interact with new cultures, you distance yourself just a little from your own. This detachment allows you to look both fondly and critically at where you come from and what you have known to be "normal" about your own way of life. If you allow the trivial details of everyday life to overwhelm your thoughts and negatively consume your energy then you can easily miss everything else around you. Opening yourself up to the people and places around you as you travel adds perspective and enrichment. I hope that this book brings just a little bit of that perspective and awe about a part of the world that is rapidly regaining recognition and attention as it emerges from its own historical turbulence.

Nick Rowan, March 2020

A boy flies a kite in Bukhara's old town centre.

Handcrafted Uzbek puppets at the ready in Bukhara.

The majestic turquoise dome of the Po-i-Kalyan mosque in Bukhara serenely silhouettes against a perfect sunset.

A spice vendor's view of Bukhara's Kalyan minaret. This prominent structure, part of the Po-i-Kalyan mosque complex, was built in 1127 by the Kharakhanid ruler, Mohammad Arslan Khan, reaching over 45 metres tall. In times of war this minaret was used as a military watchtower to scout for potential enemy movements

ACKNOWLEDGEMENTS

This book has been over ten years in the making. It has finally gotten over the publishing hurdle that is trying to bring a text and accompanying photos together in a harmonious, relevant and engaging way. Although the book bears my name, it quite simply would never have gotten off the ground without the tremendous contributions of folk, old and new, who all played their part in bringing the Silk Road alive through this publication.

Thanks are firstly due to Marat Akhmedjanov who, as a publisher of all things Central Asia, believed in the concept, trusted me with the text and then provided the resources and tools to bring it all together into this magnificent publication. Right beside Marat, in every way, is Alexandra Vlasova, who designed the layout with her usual professionalism and expertise, enabling me to input my vision, but expertly guiding me to the final result. This, in addition, to our great friendship cultivated over many years and many different projects.

For the text, my editor, Paul Robert Walker, deserves special mention for really assisting me in turning sometimes muddled ideas in to proper content, providing additional research and encouraging me to persevere with the text.

For the photographs I make special mention to the members of the Eurasian Creative Guild who kindly provided their photographs that they felt reflected the traditions and history of the Silk Road as it exists today. They did so voluntarily. The book would be little more than an essay without them and the diversity of themes and people make the book all the richer. Special mention for providing numerous photographs and input goes to: Feruz Rustamov, Mukhhiddin A Lee,Dovlet Madadov, Eduard Kamenskih, James Stronsky,Zeinulla Kakimzhanov, Nina V. Belomestnova,Pavel Svoboda, Dan Lundberg, İhsan Gerçelman & others.

Finally, I have my family to thank, who have put up with "Daddy" heading off into his study to write on many an occasion. To my daughters, Olivia and Matilda, who would provide moments of relief during difficult sessions and to my wife, Deborah, who has put up with my never ceasing fascination with Central Asia and the Silk Road, enabling me to continue writing and travelling - thank you, thank you, thank you.

A nomadic family's yurts sit serenely on a plateau of Kyrgyzstan's grasslands ready for the summer season. Many Kyrgyz are revitalising their nomadic traditions as a means of living more sustainably in the face of climate change.

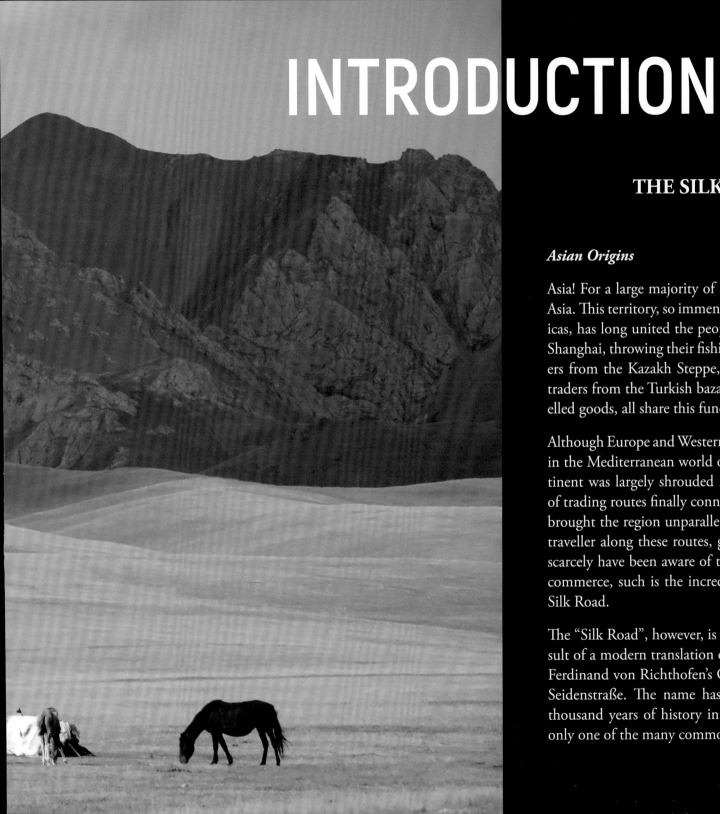

INTRODUCTION

THE SILK ROAD TODAY

Asian Origins

Asia! For a large majority of mankind, there is no other world but Asia. This territory, so immense that it equals the area of both Americas, has long united the people who live upon it. Fishermen from Shanghai, throwing their fishing nets into the East China Sea, hunters from the Kazakh Steppe, riding their horses in the wind, and traders from the Turkish bazaars, even today selling their well-travelled goods, all share this fundamental identity of the Old World.

Although Europe and Western Asia had plenty of early contact within the Mediterranean world of antiquity, the rest of the Asian continent was largely shrouded in mystery until an intricate network of trading routes finally connected East and West. These trade lines brought the region unparalleled fame and wealth. Yet the ordinary traveller along these routes, going about his daily business, would scarcely have been aware of the significance of his movements and commerce, such is the incredible story of the development of the Silk Road.

The "Silk Road", however, is an unfortunate misnomer. It is the result of a modern translation of nineteenth-century historian Baron Ferdinand von Richthofen's German term for these trading routes, Seidenstraße. The name has come to symbolize more than two thousand years of history in this part of the world, but it evokes only one of the many commodities that were traded. Silk may have been the most enticing and beguiling of materials, but other items from gold to ivory, glass to gunpowder, and exotic animals to medicinal plants were also passed along the Road. While silk production, once the world's best kept and most intriguing secret, ultimately led to the connection between China and Rome, the trade routes of Asia had been active for centuries before Chinese silk reached the West.

Except for the famous Polo family, and a few other extraordinary adventurers, merchants did not travel the entire length of the Silk Road. To do so would have risked long periods of the merchants' lives on a single shipment that, if not thieved along the way, would seldom compensate for the enormous investment of time and effort. Instead, merchants made relatively short journeys between cities, along familiar pathways, trading their goods at each place along the way. Some goods of particularly high value did travel the whole length of the road in this manner, but most reached more local or regional destinations.

There was, therefore, never one single road, but rather an intricate arterial network of roads, forming the conduits that facilitated commerce across Europe and Asia. This invisible river of commerce and exchange left behind great wealth that led to the architectural marvels that line the Silk Road today. While there is no evidence of a Roman presence in China, nor of a Chinese presence in Rome, their goods were enjoyed in both places. So entwined were these regions that Roman orator, Cicero, noted ominously, that "the credit of the Roman money-market is intimately bound up with the prosperity of Asia; a disaster cannot occur there without shaking our credit to its foundations". For more than a thousand years the Silk Road was the most important trade route in the world.

Top: A silkworm cocoon is broken open to reveal the carcass of its creator. A single cocoon can provide between 300 and 900 metres of fine silk thread.

Bottom: Beautifully decorated silks, rolled and stacked, await sale at a traditional silk merchant's stall, in China.

The Silk Road Legacy

While trade was the Silk Road's primary objective, its true glory and unique contribution to our history was the exchange of ideas, arts, technologies, and religions that occurred among the very different cultures that used it, as well as the inception of political lines of communication still in operation today. It is along the network of these trading routes that the original "globalisation" became defined. In our modern age, it may seem perfectly normal that we can interact with people from all over the world across the Internet and exchange information, ideas, and traditions at the click of a button from our armchairs. But, the fact that trade and communication thrived over these distances two thousand years ago is remarkable.

Asia is the ancestral cradle for all the principal world religions—from Judaism, with its pure-in-spirit prophets, to Buddhism, with its philosophy of enlightenment; from Christianity, with its message of love, to Islam, with its discipline and charity. The prophets of these religions were born in Asia and preached their revelations there, yet it was Silk Road merchants (along with the occasional invading army) who carried these beliefs throughout the continent. The Zoroastrian tradition, which originated in the first millennium B.C. and spread throughout the Persian Empire, directly influenced Judaism, Christianity, and Islam. Its founder was a lonely traveller named Zarathustra, who carried poetic treatises about the oneness of God along the same dusty and dangerous roads of Middle Asia that would later be travelled by Silk Road merchants. Traditional Buddhism came from India to China along the Road, merging with Taoism from the east. All these religions co-existed and mingled

A giant statue of Buddha watches over the faithful in China. Originating in ancient India between the 4th and 6th centuries B.C., before spreading throughout Asia along the Silk Road, it is now the fourth largest world religion with over 500 million followers seeking to attain Nirvana and escape the cycle of death and rebirth.

more or less peacefully. Their ideas have formed the basis of civilisation as we know it today.

Along with these religions, many other new horizons of knowledge, from architecture to astronomy, opened up as a direct consequence of trade along the Silk Road. Although they were unaware of the significance of their travels, these merchants' footprints left behind cultural transformations, new scientific ideas, and a material wealth not seen previously in Middle Asia. The Silk Road today is littered with examples of this melting pot of nations and philosophies, forming the foundations of contemporary society. You cannot link the political map to the ethnic map of real life – it constantly diverges unexpectedly. Despite this mixture of potentially conflicting ideologies, the era of the Silk Road often saw racial, religious, and cultural differences put aside for the advancement of trade. There were battles for control of the routes in any given region, but there was also an understanding that cooperation was necessary to keep the Silk Road open.

The Great Playing Field

During the nineteenth century, after several centuries of European neglect and disinterest, the Silk Road region once again took centre stage as the playing field for the "Great Game". This strategic effort for the expansion of territories and power was fuelled by the imperial rivalries and ambitions of the nineteenth-century Russian and British Empires. As the Russians expanded into Central Asia and the British sought to influence Afghanistan and Tibet, each side used the promise of renewed trade and diplomatic relations to persuade local tribespeople to give their allegiance. The outcome of this contest led to the creation of the Soviet states south of Russia and to Afghanistan and Pakistan's final demarcation.

The Pamir Mountains (often called the "Heart of Asia" and the "Roof of the World") are situated in the very centre of the Silk Road and became a focal point for the Russians. The Great Turan lowland, which spreads out from the base of this mountain system, today includes most of Uzbekistan, Kyrgyzstan, Kazakhstan, Turkmenistan and parts of Tajikistan. These now-independent countries were formed as a result of events that took place between 1924-5. Central Asia was firmly within Russia's grasp, and it was a time of intensive artificial demarcation to create national republics as part of the Soviet state. In February 1925 constitutive meetings of the Uzbek and Turkmen Soviet Socialist Republics (SSR) elected their governments and signed declarations joining the USSR. After further partitioning, the Tajik SSR was formed in 1929 followed by the Kirgyz and Kazakh SSRs in 1936.

Far left: The exquisitely painted ceiling of the Chora Museum in Istanbul envelopes Christian worshippers. Often seen as a faith of foreign travelling merchants, Christianity travelled along the Silk Road and splintered into several minority groups including Assyrian Christians, Nestorian Christians and Eastern Christians.

Near left: A stone carving (circa 515 B.C.) from the Apadana Palace's northern stairway in Persepolis, Iran, shows Persian soldiers wearing rectangular hats and Median soldiers wearing round hats.

Above: The wild and rugged mountains of the Silk Road often forced travellers to take circuitous routes or face hardship and danger crossing mountain passes.

Rediscovery and Plunder

Even one hundred years ago, educated and cultured Europeans considered the Asian continent mysterious and enigmatic. The very name, "Silk Road," evoked adventure and danger, wrapped within the exotic and mystical. The numerous scientific expeditions that left for Asia around the turn of the twentieth century, braved insuperable challenges, hardships, and death in order to re-discover the glory and majesty of the past. The closed cities of Arabia, China, Tibet, and India surpassed all imagination for those who dared visit. With some of the world's most ancient civilizations born and developed in the Asian "cradle," the region presented a goldmine of cultural treasures and insight into the origins of human development. Intrepid researchers from Europe quickly discovered a different philosophy and new cultural shape. Yet this intriguing world seemed both familiar and congenial, like their native home, a place where the first conceptions about the world had been grown.

During these early twentieth century expeditions, famous explorers such as Sven Hedin, Sir Aurel Stein, and Albert Von Le Coq began to remove the treasures they'd discovered buried along the Silk Road within the context of scientific study. As a result of their "research," physical remnants of the historic Silk Road are now scattered throughout the globe, and spectacular artefacts can be found in the British Museum in London, the National Museum in Delhi, and the Museum of Indian Art in West Berlin. Fortunately, not all the treasures were removed before local governments began prohibiting such cultural plunder, and exquisite art and other testaments to past glory can still be found *in situ*, along the fabled Silk Road where they were first created.

A restored section of the Great Wall just outside Beijing snakes across the verdant countryside. Built to protect against invasions from the north in China, stretching almost 4000 miles in length, it consists of multiple segments built by different ruling dynasties, rather than being one continuous and uniform wall.

New Roads, New Horizons

The "Silk Road" of today is a manifestly different proposition from what merchants, missionaries, and explorers faced more than a thousand years ago. The once-rugged dirt tracks and mountain passes that meandered through Central Asia have been replaced by paved and tarmac roads. Flow of goods has never been easier, although some roads have lacked maintenance over the years, allowing the underlying rock to protrude through once more like a ragged window into the past.

Recent infrastructure projects have focused on improving these vital lines of transport and communication to ensure that they continue to provide an economical, safe, and ecologically friendly transit route. Investors from China, Iran, and the United States, along with local governments and private enterprises, have ploughed billions into establishing modern transport links through the rugged lands of Central Asia. In the towering mountains of Tajikistan, the effort to dig a five-kilometre tunnel at the Anzob Pass was one of many foreign participation projects to renovate the 30,000 kilometres of roads in the country, among the most mountainous in the world. Now complete, it provides year-round access from the Tajik capital of Dushanbe, in the south, to the northern Tajik and Uzbek cities of Khujand, Tashkent, and Samarkand. It reduces reliance on its volatile neighbour and paves the way for a direct road network from Iran through Herat in western Afghanistan, Mazar-i-Sharif in northern Afghanistan through Tajikistan and out to China.

Tajikistan is not alone in its development. A "New Silk Road" that follows much the same path as the old one is being created again, throughout Asia. All the countries of the Silk Road are gradually replacing infrastructure and making it easier for trucks, laden with goods, to sputter along their highways. Despite these attempts, in these rugged and often inhospitable lands, snow will always fall on 3,000-metre mountain passes, and rivers will occasionally overflow, washing away manmade constructions.

The new "Silk Railroad" continues to develop as railway lines provide a faster, more secure transport routes throughout Asia. Although the full potential of this mode of transport has yet to be realised, optimism remains that this infrastructure will further bind nations of the old Silk Road in trade and transport

The shifting desert sands of the Taklamakan Desert will continue to cover roads, reminding us that nature remains the ultimate force along the Silk Road, shaping life and travel, as it has for more than two thousand years.

On the Rails – The Silk Railroad

Two thousand years ago, goods transported along the Silk Road from China to Europe might take well over a year to reach their consumers. Today it takes barely two weeks thanks to huge stretches of steel railway line that now cling to the mountains, plains, and deserts. It is the basis for a new "Iron Silk Road" or "Silk Railroad" that comprises over 100,000 kilometres serving almost 30 countries directly.

The concept of a Trans-Asian Railway to provide a 14,000-kilometre link between Singapore and Istanbul has been beckoning since the 1960s. A Trans-Asian Railway network has been heralded by many as the key to huge increases in Eurasian trade by facilitating the movement of goods to, from, and through the landlocked countries of Central Asia. By 2006, seventeen nations had signed the United Nations Economic and Social Commission for Asia and the Pacific (UNESCAP) agreement to build this transcontinental railway. Still, progress has been slow, as differences in rail gauge, signalling systems, and railway electrification have prevented unanimous participation. Additions to the railway dream have been piecemeal, often made in the interests of the host nation rather than the continental vision. Consequently, the economic promises of a united network have yet to be fully realised.

History in the Making

A struggle for political influence is re-emerging on the plains of Central Asia. While perhaps there is less imperial gusto than there was during Russia and Britain's Great Game, nonetheless West and East are again meeting at the crossroads of Central Asia in a story that focuses on oil and gas rather than silks and spices.

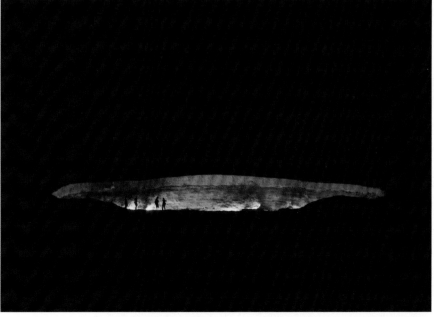

Energy security and access to new mineral deposits are providing world leaders with incentives to explore the Silk Road once again. A complex network of pipelines for delivering oil and gas to the global marketplace are being built with hurried speed. Those countries through which this oil flows will receive not only the billions of dollars in transit fees but also control over the flow. Since the end of 2009, the regional balance of power has shifted with the opening of the Central Asia-China pipeline that opened up a new market for Central Asian gas, breaking the Russian monopoly and introducing new export options. As Chinese demand for gas continues to grow over the next few decades, diversifying its import sources to spread its supply risk will be critical for its stability.

These new "Silk Road" pipelines will play a vital role in shaping the geopolitical atmosphere in Central Asia and beyond. The outcome of this oil diplomacy may very well determine the geopolitical future of the countries and peoples along the Silk Road. A new Great Game has begun in earnest, and the history of the Silk Road is by no means over – indeed maybe we are only just beginning to witness the return of the world's central power to where it ruled from for millennia.

Resurrection and Rebuilding

Following the collapse of the Soviet Union in the early 1990s, interest and attention to the restoration of the Silk Road began to increase. Central Asia provided the focus for rebuilding efforts because it was considered the heart of the ancient caravan road. As a result, its governments have been the chief initiators of international actions for the restoration of the ancient road. High-ranking delegations from all Silk Road countries have taken part in numerous international conferences to exchange opinions and ideas. The general aim of the conferences has been to gather current information and define what practical measures are necessary for revival of Silk Road networks through China, Central Asia, the Caucasus, and Europe.

Top left: Oil rig silhouettes adorn the skyline near Baku in Azerbaijan.

Bottom Left: The Darvaza gas crater, also known as the Gates of Hell, is the result of a collapsed gas field intentionally set alight in the 1970s to burn out but still burns today. The crater is located in Darvaza, Turkmenistan.

Above: At the southern end of Independence Park, a giant golden statue of Saparmyrat Niyazov also known as Turkmenbashi, Turkmenistan's first president, stands before the Monument to the Independence of Turkmenistan. The five-headed eagle represents the five provinces of Turkmenistan.

Meanwhile, historic cities have started to boom. New airports, luxury hotels and restored landmarks have all started to appear, catering for a new wave of businessmen and tourists. Oil money has allowed leaders of the Silk Road countries to lavish their countries with modern designs and ambitious (if somewhat wasteful) projects: gargantuan fountains in the desert city of Ashgabat, monumental flaming glass towers in Baku and space-age palaces and shopping centres in Astana (recently renamed Nur-Sultan).

Since 2013, China has latched onto this idea in a significant way. Although arguably Central Asia played the biggest role in the Silk Road's long history, the Chinese have almost monopolised the concept of reviving this trading route through Chinese President, Xi Jinping's, 2013 "Belt and Road Initiative" or BRI - a development strategy to reconnect the region economically through a China-centred trading network. The project has targeted completion by 2049, which happens to coincide with the 100th anniversary of the People's Republic of China.

If successful, the BRI will construct a substantial and unified market to bring capital inflows, exchange of goods and development of better cultural understanding through closer integration of China, Central Asia, India and Europe. In short, it is a resurrection and rejuvenation of enormous scale that reminds us just how important the concept of a Silk Road was before and can be again.

A River Through the Trail of Time

The Silk Road has lost none of the charm and character that it assembled over more than two thousand years. The traditions and heritage of the Silk Road are still vividly visible, and its impact on forming and developing civilisation is incomparable. Just as in the days of Marco Polo's travels, Asia remains one of the most beautiful, cultured, and energetic regions on the planet. Even today, a visit to the lively Sunday Market in

Kashgar, China, reveals age-old craftsmanship bartered in a swarming, smoky atmosphere. Driving through the fertile Fergana Valley in Uzbekistan, the ancient mulberry trees—the food source for the humble but legendary silkworm—evoke the sense of prosperity that the Silk Road once gave rise to.

However, the region is also one of the most intimidating, misunderstood, and unforgiving areas to the unprepared traveller. The vast expanses of the Taklamakan, Karakum, and Gobi Deserts, coupled with the daunting peaks of the Pamir, Karakorum, and Tien Shan Mountains, have presented even the most ambitious humankind with significant challenges since the dawn of time. Today, in areas where modern transportation infrastructure is still in the early stages of development, the challenges continue to abound.

Despite the challenges of the landscape, the verdant valleys, arid deserts, and gruelling mountain passes of this region gave rise to unprecedented trade opportunities between East and West for more than two thousand years, leaving behind a colourful array of people of extraordinary kindness and zest for life. Anyone who ventures along the Silk Road today will find that, above all, it is the people along its length about whom the history—and the legend—of the Silk Road have been built upon. Irrespective of the political and economic situation, it is the people who provide the real treat for anyone bold enough to open themselves to travel. The chapters that follow try to retell just some of their magnificent stories.

Left: The striking silhouette of the Poi-i-Kalyann mosque in Bukhara.

Right: Sunrise over the Aydarkul lake in Uzbekistan, as viewed from the warmth of a traditional nomadic yurt. The nomads were key to the development of the Silk Road and several Silk Road countries continue to embrace the nomadic way of life today, at least in part.

The banks of the Grand Canal are lined with more than 170 buildings, most of which date from the 13th to the 18th century, and demonstrate the wealth and art created by the Republic of Venice. Amongst the many are the Palazzi Barbaro, Ca' Rezzonico, Ca' d'Oro, Palazzo Dario, Ca' Foscari, Palazzo Barbarigo and the Palazzo Venier dei Leoni, housing the Peggy Guggenheim Collection.

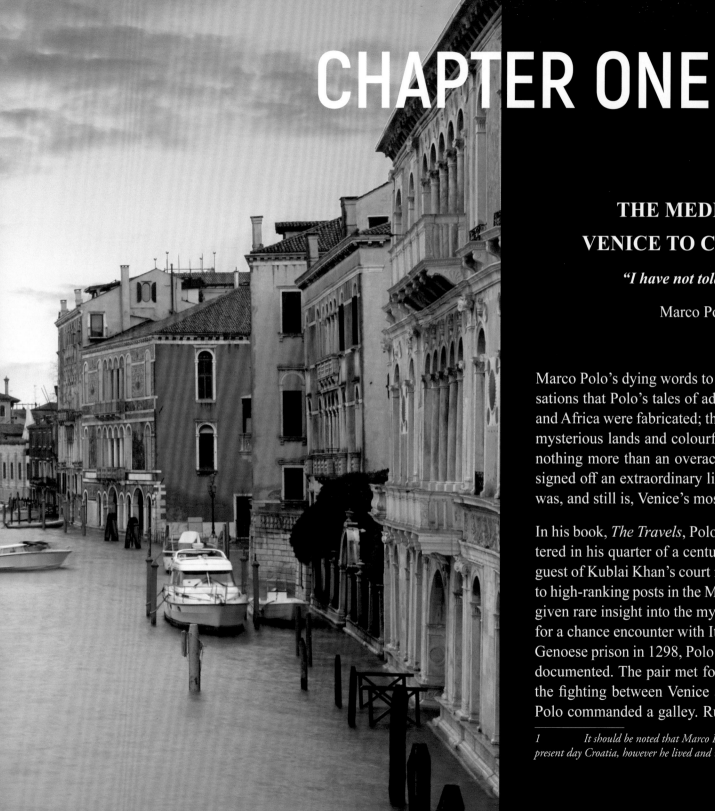

CHAPTER ONE

THE MEDITERRANEAN:
VENICE TO CONSTANTINOPLE

"I have not told half of what I saw."

Marco Polo c.1254-1324

Marco Polo's dying words to a priest were meant to answer accusations that Polo's tales of adventures in China, Mongolia, India, and Africa were fabricated; that his enchanting descriptions of the mysterious lands and colourful characters of the Silk Road were nothing more than an overactive imagination. Nonetheless, they signed off an extraordinary life of travel along the Silk Road. He was, and still is, Venice's most famous son[1].

In his book, *The Travels*, Polo recounts the splendours he encountered in his quarter of a century of travel across Asia. A welcome guest of Kublai Khan's court in China, Marco Polo was appointed to high-ranking posts in the Mongol emperor's administration and given rare insight into the mysterious workings of the East. If not for a chance encounter with Italian writer Rustichello da Pisa in a Genoese prison in 1298, Polo's adventures might never have been documented. The pair met following Marco Polo's capture amid the fighting between Venice and rival city Genoa, during which Polo commanded a galley. Rustichello's accounts of Polo's trav-

---

1 *It should be noted that Marco Polo was actually born on the island of Korcula in present day Croatia, however he lived and worked in Venice which became his adopted home.*

els in exotic lands and their untold wealth quickly became popular in a curious Europe on the cusp of its own Renaissance.

With success came doubt, and there were plenty of critics who viewed the tales with suspicion, labelling the book, *Il Milione* (The Million Lies). The lack of references to obvious landmarks such as the Great Wall of China and subjects like Chinese calligraphy and tea, as well as the book's inclusion of several far-fetched encounters, continues to raise questions today. Regardless, the book had a profound effect and influence on geographers of the time and instigated a desire for further exploration of the trading lands that lay to the east. Today there are more than eighty versions of the original manuscript, translated into a multitude of world languages.

A Fleet at the Ready

By the time Marco Polo died in 1324 at the age of 69, Venice was a well-established trading centre and the Mediterranean's dominant maritime city. The Venetian fleet was the city's most reliable weapon, capable of transporting men, supplies, and goods ever-increasing distances, thereby extending Venice's influence with its trading partners.

Venetian affinity for naval matters equalled its affinity for trade. Merchant ships were quickly transformed into warships in times of need. The skilled crews shifted between merchant and military personnel seamlessly. Before the 1400s and the widespread use of gunpowder, such agility and cunning were critical to ward off threatening pirates and control the Adriatic Sea. With control, trade could flourish. And where trade leads, cultures follow.

Many of Venice's side canals are havens of tranquility, with an unhurried way of life that charms and refreshes visitors breaking away from the main thoroughfares.

Venice's early inhabitants were refugees from northern Italy who fled to the islands of the Venetian lagoon as the Western Roman Empire fell to invaders in the fifth century A.D. This shallow body of water was protected from invasion by the numerous treacherous marshes and water channels. The islanders became expert sailors, fishermen, and tradesmen, trading both fish and salt up and down the Adriatic coast. The inhabitants formed townships that, by the end of the seventh century, led to the creation of a people's assembly led by an elected *doge*. By the fifteenth century, Venetian trade had evolved into a far more sophisticated and far-reaching endeavour.

Beginning at the End

Trade along the Silk Road is commonly misconceived as starting from Xian, China, and ending in Venice, Italy, as though it were a one-way thoroughfare. In truth, the Silk Road never started in any *one* place. A network of trade arteries grew slowly, building gradually East-West as merchants traded from village to village, valley to valley and town to town. As Chinese and European trade expanded, merchants from each side of the world, and all points in between, likely met in neighbouring regions. The end of one country's trade relations was the beginning of the next, both formally and informally.

The Silk Road was a formidable network, spanning over 5,000 miles in both directions, diverted only by war, pestilence, economy, and the bandits who quickly pounced on any opportunity to share in the merchants' riches. While Venice was situated at the westernmost point of the Silk Road, it was by no means the only receiving outpost in Europe – but it was, perhaps, the most famous.

The beauty of Venice lies in its details, such as the many fascinating doorknobs that add grandeur to Venetian houses, transforming them into grand palazzos. Doorknobs became popular in Venice in 1546 after Jacobo Sansovino designed a bold new bronze door for the Basilica di San Marco decorated with six heads depicting, amongst others, himself and the painter Tiziano.

Through the Venetian Looking Glass

As it developed a reputation for intricate and colourful glasswork, Venice began to export this commodity along with silver, wool, and even timber. The quality of glass workmanship was so high that Venice, for many centuries, held an unrivalled monopoly on glassmaking. The craft was largely concentrated on the island of Murano, one-and-a-half kilometres north of Venice's main islands in the lagoon, after the Venetian Republic ordered the destruction of all foundries in the city—fearing the significant fire hazard these workshops posed to a city largely constructed out of wood.

On Murano, technological advances in glassmaking were made with such alacrity that Venice's competitive advantage remained strong and demand for its product grew. Improvements to the glass's colour, transparency, and decoration meant that the changing fashions of high society were always satisfied. By the fourteenth century, glassmakers were some of the most affluent citizens of Venice.

Eastern Influence in Venice and Beyond

The import of luxurious, high-value goods and ideas from the East greatly impacted European society from Venice to London. The influx of foreign goods changed the lives of even the most ordinary of citizens. Cooking became more exotic as spices such as saffron, nutmeg, and cinnamon were imported from the East, and music and theatre was equally "spiced" with new ideas from foreign lands. Medicine adopted previously unheard of remedies.

Exquisite examples of hand blown Venetian glassware on sale in Murano, Italy.

Until the middle of the fifteenth century, the Venetian republic and its neighbouring city states had significant control on the silk and spice trade between Central Asia and Europe. Venice became a formidable power over all aspects of trade, with Venetian merchants acting as the middlemen for the Western world. Paintings from the Renaissance capture in loving detail the bright colours of silks, velvets and carpets that reflect the growth of Eastern-influenced marketplaces in the city.

Eastern influences also shaped Venice's skyline. Walking through the city today, it is not hard to find examples of Eastern design and décor as a reminder of the foundations upon which it was built. Once aware of these influences, even the most casual of visitors begins to notice them everywhere. Perhaps the most striking are the marble facades of the Palazzo Ducale (*Doge's* Palace) that dominate St Mark's Square. The brickwork patterns on these facades are startlingly similar to those seen at the base of the Kalon minaret of Bukhara in present-day Uzbekistan. Likewise, the stone-lattice windows also visible on many buildings in the city are reminiscent of those carved in the palaces of Damascus and Aleppo in Syria and the merchant buildings in India. Many other grandiose buildings, including the Palazzo Contarini del Bovolo with its exquisite external spiral staircase, reflect the Persian mosques, bazaars, and palaces that Venetian merchants once visited.

Venice's position at the head of the Adriatic was a key enabler in building extensive relationships with both the Byzantine Empire and the emerging Muslim world. But the city was not simply a marketplace profiting economically from trade; it was actively digesting and emulating the Eastern cultures it encountered through that trade. With the goods came the people selling them, who in turn brought their own beliefs, ideas, and technologies that benefited and changed Venetian society.

The serene courtyard of the Palazzo Ducale, also known as the Doge's Palace in Venice, Italy.

A view from the Grand Canal of the Doge's Palace and St Mark's Square in Venice, Italy.

Venice on the World Stage

Venice's affluence drew great jealousy from other cities and states. Venice, and other city states, including Pisa and Genoa, understood that their naval prowess enabled them to form and control relationships with Dalmatian Coast cities such as Dubrovnik and Split to benefit from trade locally and access the lands beyond. It was the Italian city states who immediately seized on the fact that their fleets could provide a pivotal role for the newly energised eleventh century Crusaders' ambitions on holy Jerusalem.

The Crusaders' success, as they ventured further from Europe, depended on adequate provisioning from European cities – not only did this require a logistical fleet of ships but the ability to siege ports along the littoral ports of the holy land such as Jaffa, Caesarea and Acre. After generous terms had been secured for their help, the Venetians and Genoese fortunes were transformed at a dizzying rate. No longer were they regional power houses, they were now international power houses.

Constantinople's Silken Secrets

By the middle of the twelfth century, the Italian city states were the envy of all others in Europe. They had brilliantly and creatively used their power to gain unparalleled wealth and status. However soon after, the relationship between Venice and another Silk Road terminus city, Constantinople (modern-day Istanbul), had become strained through a series of diplomatic incidents involving Constantinople's arrest of visiting Venetians. Furthermore, Constantinople's citizens had begun to begrudge the privileges that the Venetians took in order to enjoy their newfound wealth, especially as the two states used similar trading routes in their pursuit of the luxurious goods of the East.

Santa Maria della Salute church in Venice, sanctioned during the devastating plague outbreak in 1630 in a bid for divine protection.

Located on the European side of the narrow Bosporus Strait that separates Europe and Asia, Constantinople was even better situated than Venice to control trade flowing from the Silk Road into the Mediterranean world. In the first century B.C., long before Venice existed as a city state, silk passed through Constantinople—then called Byzantium—on its way to imperial Rome. In A.D. 330, when Roman Emperor Constantine moved the capital of the empire to the city and renamed it Constantinople, it became even more powerful. It connected the Mediterranean with the Black Sea, controlling maritime traffic and trade. By land it linked not only east and west but also north and south. That power continued as it served as capital of the Eastern Roman Empire—called the Byzantine Empire—after the fall of Rome.

As the secret of silk production (or sericulture) started to leak its way out of China and into Europe by the early-sixth century A.D.— thanks, supposedly, to the smuggling efforts of Persian Christian monks—the Byzantines began to develop their own silk industry. They also acquired the rare ability to make the brilliant purple dye that was sought after throughout Europe. As a result, finely dyed silk was used to organise Byzantine hierarchical structure, for only the upper echelons of society were allowed to wear the coveted purple-dyed silk. So important was this commodity that it was also used as a gift to resolve diplomatic situations.

No matter how many cities Silk Road travellers had passed through, few had seen anything quite like Constantinople. It was virtually unmatched in size and grandeur—drawing amazement from all who entered her walls. Set on the shores of the Bosporus, this remarkably beautiful city also held special importance for the Christian world as a centre of faith. The Bishop of Constantinople was second only to the Pope from the time of Constantine until the Great Schism of 1054 that divided the Eastern, Greek-speaking Church from the Western,

Built in 500 A.D., the 67 metre tall Galata Tower in Istanbul is one of the city's dominating landmarks. Although previously a defensive watchtower, today the upper floors host a restaurant, cafe and nightclub.

Latin-speaking Church. From then onwards, Constantinople was the centre of what became known as the Eastern Orthodox Church.

Byzantine emperors devoted much energy and considerable sums of money to lavish the city with Christian monuments. Emperor Justinian I set out to establish the superiority of the Christian church by commissioning the construction of the architectural masterpiece, the Hagia Sophia, completed in 537 A.D. Constantinople provided a new epicentre of Europe as well as a gateway to Asia, forming a strategic link between East and West as it straddled the two great continents. Although its fortunes ebbed and flowed, several times it regained the title of largest and richest city in Europe.

A Changing City

Byzantium was originally founded by the Greeks, and until Constantine arrived with his Roman court, it was a decidedly Greek city. Although Constantine, and the Roman emperors who followed him, established Roman laws and culture and made Latin the official language, most inhabitants continued to speak Greek. In 610, the emperor Heraclius changed the official language back to Greek and Constantinople continued to evolve into a multi-cultural society as a result of its heritage, location, and trading connections on the Silk Road.

As the Dark Ages that beset Europe following the fall of the Roman Empire slowly came to an end, the Silk Road and Constantinople—where much of Roman knowledge had been kept alive—played a pivotal role in returning medicine, philosophy, geography and science to Western Europe. By the ninth century A.D. Arabic had been integrated into the culture of Constantinople and this new language was commonplace in the city, as it ushered in a new era of greater prosperity and wealth.

The Hagia Sophia mosque. Formerly the site of several Greek Eastern Orthodox Churches, it was later converted into a Mosque by the Ottomans and, today sits as a museum after Atatürk designated its deconsecration in 1935.

After the Byzantines lost substantial territory to invading Turkish tribes, Emperor Alexios I Komnenos (1081-1118) re-established the empire's military, financial and territorial might, recovering much of the previously lost lands in Anatolia (modern-day Turkey). However, continued threats from the Turks led to Alexios' call for support from the West that brought soldiers of the First Crusade to Constantinople and provided a temporary reprieve. Alexios was the first of the Komenenos dynasty, which extended until 1185 and brought renewed stability and a rise in trade during the twelfth century. The city's population swelled to over half a million people and its ties with the Venetians strengthened again, with such foreigners providing almost a quarter of the city's population.

Left and Above: The interior and exterior of the Blue Mosque in Istanbul. The 20,000 hand-made Izmir tiles that decorate the interior are inspired by Chinese art and ceramic techniques brought to the region by the Mongols and the later fifteenth century Ming porcelains.

The End of Empires

After diplomatic relations between Venice and Istanbul broke down again during the late twelfth century, the solidarity in trade and power never fully recovered. Venice launched the Fourth Crusade in 1203, blessed by Pope Innocent III, but instead of reaching the Holy Land, the Crusaders first diverted to attack Constantinople. In 1204, the Latin Christian Crusaders breached the sea walls and pillaged the city of the proud Greek Christians. Many cultural treasures of the former capital of Christian civilisation were taken away or destroyed. It was an indescribably cruel sacking that unambiguously revealed the European frame of mind – they would stop at nothing from getting closer to the power and riches they so craved. The sack of the city was an unparalleled disaster from which Constantinople never fully recovered. The schism between the Greek and Latin churches was not only widened but irreparably complete. The weakened Byzantine imperial apparatus was now rapidly becoming easy prey for further Muslim conquests of Anatolia and the Balkans in the centuries to come.

Almost three hundred years later, in 1498, the news of Portuguese Vasco da Gama's successful sea voyage to India consigned Venetian and Byzantine mercantile power to the shadows of Silk Road history. His discovery of an abundance of spices in the coastal town of Calicut (modern day Kozhikode in the state of Kerala, India) shocked the inhabitants of both cities to the core.

This newly discovered maritime route enabled da Gama to sell spices for sixty times the price he had paid for them. Venice and its neighbours could not compete with the Portuguese, who could now carry their spices straight to Lisbon for sale in European markets, avoiding the taxes and lengthy travels along the Silk Road that inflated Venetian-traded goods by up to one hundred times their original cost. The news of the Portuguese success led Venetian noble and merchant diarist, Girolamo Priuli, to write, "I clearly see the ruin of the city of Venice."

In truth, the Venetian Republic's power had already greatly diminished by this point. With a weakened Constantinople defeated in 1453 by the Ottomans under Mehmet the Conqueror, Europeans were effectively cut out of the prosperous Silk Road trade. Blocked from using the combined sea and land routes of the past, they had to pay heavy taxes in order to access the silks and spices they had grown so dependent upon. Unable to compete with the Portuguese and Spanish ocean-going ships that now dominated the East, the Europeans looked south to Africa for a new source of trade, but their power and influence never again reached the heights of those golden Silk Road days.

The spectacular Lycian funerary tombs near Fethiye, Turkey, were carved into the mountainside in the fifth century B.C. The Lycians believed a mythical winged creature would carry them off into the afterlife, hence the position of the tombs on cliffs.

Constantinople (Istanbul) Today

Nowhere else in today's world do history and geography merge so dramatically as in Istanbul. Its unique gateway position remains beautifully defined by the mile-long Bosporus suspension bridge—the true "land bridge" connecting Europe with Asia—that opened in 1973.

Istanbul embodies the meeting of East and West like nowhere else. The Hagia Sophia—first a Byzantine Christian church and then an Ottoman mosque, and still revered by both religions today—demonstrates just how critical a nexus this city was to the Silk Road's development. Even though it is firmly enshrined as a secular place today, favouring neither religion as is representative of Turkey's own political position until very recently, Istanbul has lost none of its grandeur and substance from the religious influences of its past.

If the architecture of Istanbul is breathtaking, then the development and commerce of its bazaars is truly overwhelming. These sprawling undercover markets, with their narrow alleyways brimming in every corner with brightly coloured produce and handicrafts in the dim, smoke-filled light, are glimpses at what once provided this Silk Road city with its prominence and prosperity.

A visit to Istanbul's Grand Bazaar still evokes the Silk Road era with the constant murmur of industrious bartering, the heady scents that ascend from exotic spices and the engulfing invasion of colour and pattern from the alluring carpets and clothes hung out in front of shops. Istanbul is fast reasserting itself as a financial and trading centre, and the buzz of commerce echoes once more in its hallowed alleyways and beyond.

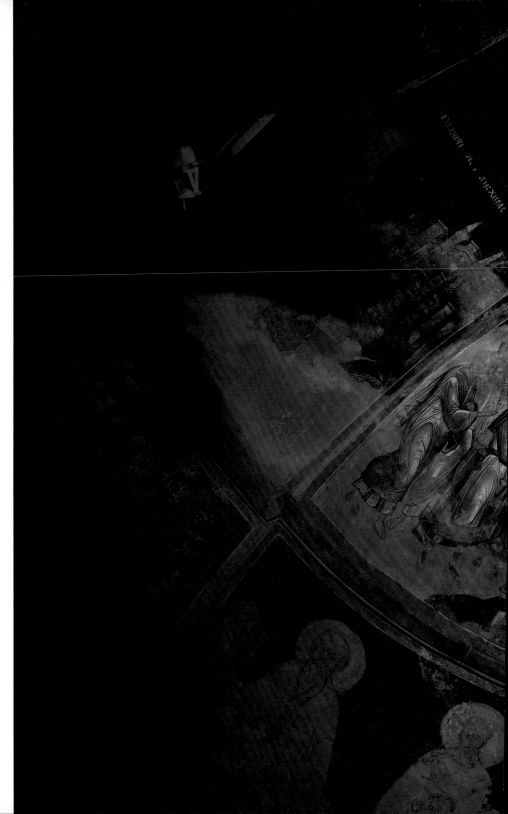

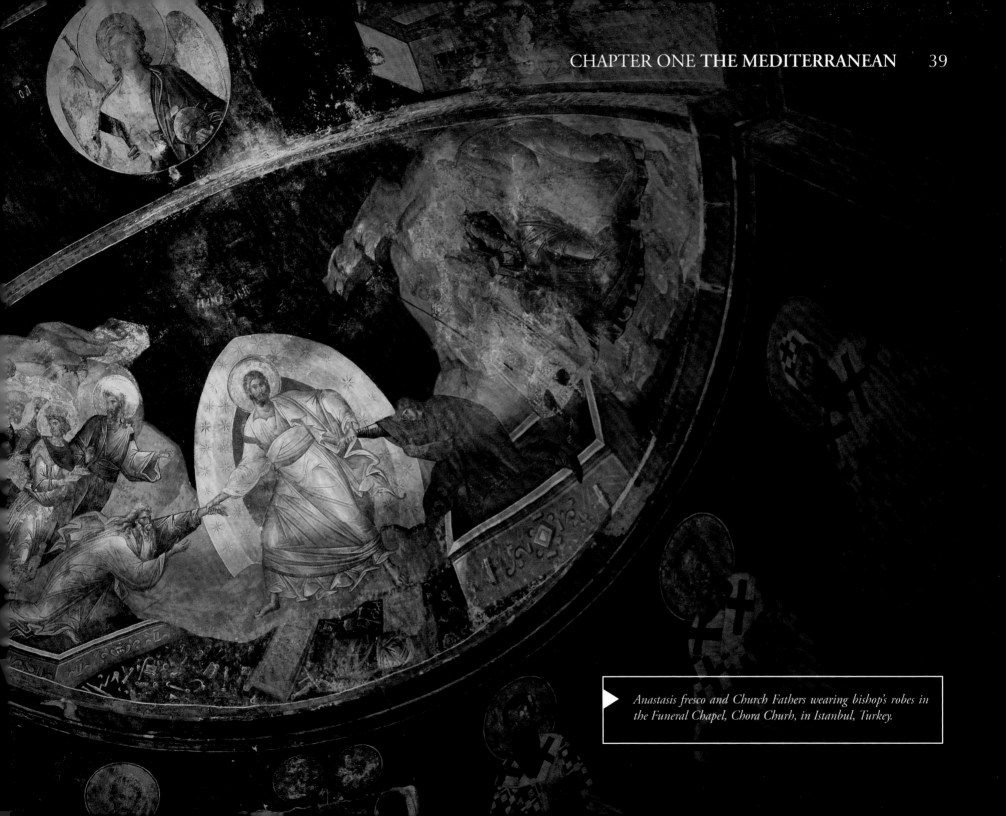

Anastasis fresco and Church Fathers wearing bishop's robes in the Funeral Chapel, Chora Churh, in Istanbul, Turkey.

> Tea is the most commonly consumed hot drink in Turkey, acting as a key ingredient in social and commercial interaction. Traditionally offered to guests in small tulip-shaped glasses, tea drinkers usually hold the rim of the glass to avoid fingertips being burned from the boiling hot liquid.

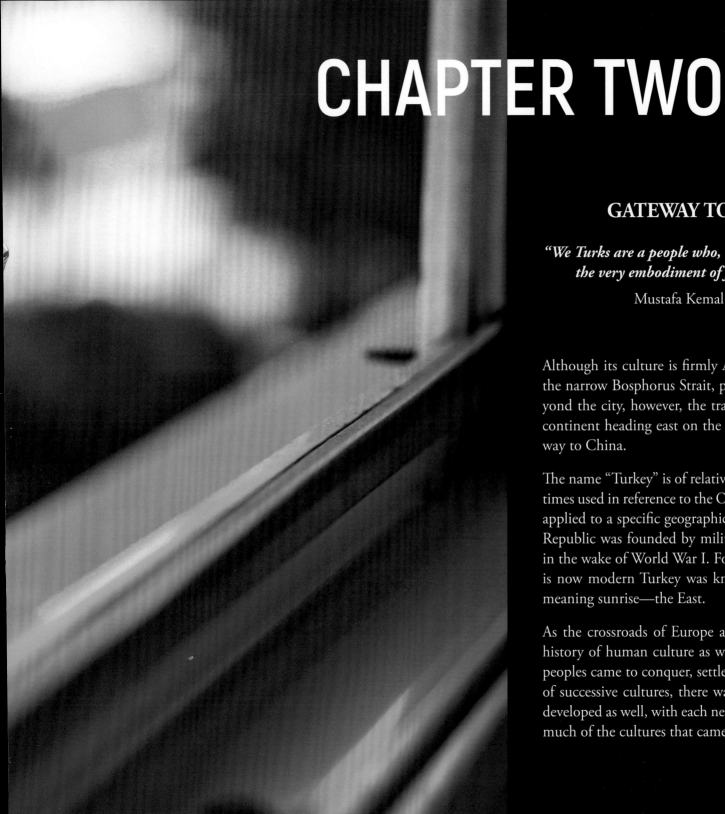

CHAPTER TWO

GATEWAY TO ASIA: TURKEY

"We Turks are a people who, throughout our history, have been the very embodiment of freedom and independence."

Mustafa Kemal Atatürk 1881-1938

Although its culture is firmly Asian, the city of Istanbul straddles the narrow Bosphorus Strait, part in Europe and part in Asia. Beyond the city, however, the traveller moves deeper into the Asian continent heading east on the ancient Silk Road that leads all the way to China.

The name "Turkey" is of relatively modern origin. Although sometimes used in reference to the Ottoman Empire, it was not officially applied to a specific geographic area until 1923, when the Turkish Republic was founded by military officer Mustafa Kemal Ataturk in the wake of World War I. For much of its history, most of what is now modern Turkey was known by its Greek name, Anatolia, meaning sunrise—the East.

As the crossroads of Europe and Asia, Anatolia fashioned a rich history of human culture as wave after wave of wave of disparate peoples came to conquer, settle, and trade. Yet, despite the overlay of successive cultures, there was a remarkable social stability that developed as well, with each new culture adopting and assimilating much of the cultures that came before them.

An Ancient Land

Testimony to this ancient history are the excavations at Çatalhüyük in southern Anatolia (near present-day Konya), where archaeologists have discovered the remains of what may be the world's first city, dating at least to 6,500 B.C. and probably earlier. After rising to a population of almost 10,000, the city disappeared around 5,700 B.C., but the culture of Anatolia continued to develop.

From 2500 to 2000 B.C., the art of metallurgy began to flourish, first with copper and then with bronze. Assyrian merchants established trading colonies and supplied metal armour for the armies of Mesopotamia (modern day Iraq), which further developed trade on the roads to the east. Around 1800 B.C., Indo-European invaders—using war chariots drawn by powerful horses—crossed the Caucasus Mountains and conquered the central plain of Anatolia. Known as the Hittites, they embraced the culture of the local people, while establishing efficient systems of commerce and taxation. The elements of a trading network were already in place, and Hittite trade began to flourish.

Hittite rule lasted until around 1160 B.C. brought down by civil war and the threat of invasions from the sea. Various smaller states struggled for control until, around 600 B.C., when the Lydians established an empire in western Anatolia, fed by a natural alloy of silver and gold, called electrum, that was found in the Pactolus River near the Aegean coast. Using electrum initially, and later refined gold, the Lydians established the world's first coinage system, an invention that further stimulated trade. Despite their natural riches, the Lydian Empire was short-lived. In 546 B.C., Lydia's wealthy king Croesus—from whom the expression "rich as Croesus" comes—attacked the newly established Persian Empire but was defeated by its founder, Cyrus the Great. In revenge, Lydia was forced to become an extended province (satrapy) of the Persian Empire.

The impressive facade of the Library of Celsus in Ephesus, Turkey. Once the third largest library in the Roman world, its contents and structure were destroyed by a fire from an earthquake in the third century A.D. and lay in ruins until archaeologists restored the facade in the 1970s.

The Persians brought new life to Anatolian trade. By the early fifth century B.C. the Persian Royal Road ran some 2,700 kilometres from the Persian capital of Susa to the old Lydian capital of Sardis in western Anatolia. Other roads branched to the Aegean ports of Smyrna (modern Izmir) and Ephesus (now abandoned). It proved such a vital line of communication that the Persians set up a relay system of successive messengers on fast horses able to cover the route in just nine days. This prompted Greek historian Herodotus to write, "Neither snow, nor rain, nor heat, nor darkness of night prevents these couriers from completing their designated stages with utmost speed."

Susa (modern Shush, Iran) was situated 400 kilometres south of the route that would later become the Silk Road, but as the Royal Road headed to the northwest, the two routes met at Arbela (Arbil) in what is now northern Iraq and continued as one route all the way to Sardis, in western Turkey. Thus, four centuries before silk arrived from China, the western portion of the Silk Road was already established as a major thoroughfare.

The Greeks

Beginning in the third millennium B.C., the Aegean coast of Anatolia had been within the cultural influence of the highly developed Minoan civilisation on the island of Crete. Later it became part of the Greek world. The Greek invasion of Troy around 1190 B.C., even if there is some truth to the story of rescuing the beautiful Queen Helen, was probably a Greek raid on the Anatolian Coast.

According to legend, the Greek colony of Byzantium was founded in 667 B.C. by King Byzas on the present site of European Istanbul. With a strategic location controlling the Bosporus Strait—the narrowest passage on the route from the Aegean Sea to the Black Sea, the sea route from Europe to Asia—Byzantium was destined to become one the great cities of the world and a key location on the Silk Road.

A restored column protrudes proudly in Ephesus, Turkey.

In the spring of 334 B.C., in order to avenge the invasions of Greece by the Persians more than a century earlier, King Alexander of the Greek state of Macedonia led an army to attack Asia. Crossing the Hellespont (now known as the Dardanelles), another narrow water passage south of the Bosporus, they landed near Troy and, after minor resistance from the Persians, retook the Greek cities on the Aegean. Heading inland, Alexander forced a number of local princes to recognize his rule and marched along the Persian Royal Road from Ankara to Tarsus.

Alexander's forces met the Persian army, under Darius III, near the Gulf of Issus, the corner of Anatolia and Syria (near the modern city of Iskenderun, Turkey). Although the Persians had superior strength, the Greeks forced them to flee eastward towards Persia. Rather than chasing the defeated enemy, Alexander led his army on a two-year expedition through Syria, Palestine, and Egypt. Of special interest during this campaign was the purple dye made by the Phoenicians from molluscs on the Mediterranean coast. Shades of purple from this dye had become a mark of royalty, especially favoured by the Persians, and would soon become an integral part of the silk trade.

Alexander finally headed east toward Persia in 331 B.C. and spent another eight years campaigning in Persia, India, and beyond before his death in the ancient city of Babylon. He pushed as far east as the modern city of Khujand, in Tajikistan, and established his eastern capital at Bactra in what is now northern Afghanistan, the halfway point of the Silk Road and arguably one of its most important cities.

▶ *The stunning amphitheatre in the ancient city of Hierapolis, an ancient Greek city located over the hot springs in south-west Anatolia, adjacent to the modern town of Pamukkale.*

Precious Fabric

After Alexander's death, his empire was divided among his generals. The largest portion went to Seleucus Nicator, founder of the Seleucid Empire (312 B.C. – 63 B.C.). At the height of his reign Seleucus controlled a vast empire that stretched from Afghanistan into Anatolia. Despite his great holdings, the roads to the sea were blocked. Rivals controlled the ports on the Aegean coast and the Egyptian ruler Ptolemy I (another of Alexander's generals) controlled the purple dye factories in Phoenicia. In 300 B.C., faced with these barriers to trade, Seleucus built a new capital called Antioch on the Orontes River, which offered access to the Mediterranean 32 kilometres away.

Laid out on a grid with broad colonnaded avenues, Antioch (modern Antakya, Turkey) became one of the greatest cities of the Mediterranean world, on a par with Alexandria and Rome. Then considered part of Syria, it became a major western terminus of the Silk Road as well as the northern terminus of the Incense Road from Arabia.

Although we speak of the Silk Road during this period, the western part of the road that led to Antioch did not carry any substantial amount of silk until sometime after the Seleucid Empire fell to Rome in 63 B.C. Scholars disagree regarding when silk first reached Europe. Some believe that small amounts had already begun to arrive by Alexander's time, perhaps by a northern route through the steppes of Russia or by the Silk Road itself, while others believe that no silk passed through until after Chinese diplomats arrived in what is now Iran around 105 B.C. Silk apparently remained unknown to Rome until 53 B.C. when Roman soldiers

Producing silk fibers. Extracting raw silk starts by cultivating the silkworms on mulberry leaves. Once the worms start pupating in their cocoons, these are dissolved in boiling water in order for individual long fibres to be extracted and fed into the spinning reel.

were shocked and disoriented by beautifully dyed silk banners unfurled in battle by the "barbarian" Parthians who then ruled the Iranian Plateau.

Silk, as well as Asian jewels and spices, quickly gained popularity among the wealthy Romans. Then, just as the obsession gained hold, the Silk Road was all but cut off due to attacks by hostile tribes in western China. Eager to maintain the flow of luxury items, Augustus Caesar took control of the Red Sea ports of the Spice Route that brought goods from the east through the Indian Ocean. This route was much longer than the Silk Road and offered its own dangers with rough seas and attacks by pirates, but it opened up a new source of wealth that outshone silk. Nevertheless, the Roman craving for silk continued and ever higher sums of Roman coinage were being consumed in its acquisition, much to the lament of Pliny the Elder who remarked upon the cost to the economy of the silk trade in his writings. Such was the concern that the Roman financial system might suffer that, in A.D. 14, the Senate tried to prevent men from wearing it under the pretext that the soft, near-transparent material made men effeminate and was therefore dishonourable and immoral.

By the end of the first century A.D., as China regained control of its western frontier, the Silk Road was once again open for business and became the most important route for silk and other luxuries from the east. The Romans in turn sent gold, silver, and other goods along the road to the mysterious people they called the Seres, the people of silk. In fact, these goods did not really pass directly between China and Rome, but rather through a series of adventurous middlemen, whose trade raised the prices exorbitantly along the way.

Turkish glass lamps for sale in the Grand Bazaar, Istanbul.

Early Christianity

As the gateway to Asia, Anatolia and neighbouring Syria were of prime importance to Rome. The Romans continued to develop Antioch as a beautiful, impressive city and the seat of government for the region. By the fourth century A.D., Antioch had reached a population almost half a million.

Along with its strategic importance to Rome, Antioch and other cities of Anatolia became the centre of early Christianity. Led by Paul, a Greek-speaking Jew from Tarsus in southern Anatolia, early missionaries established communities at several cities in the region. According to legend, St. Peter created the first Christian church in a cave in Antioch, which is still used as a church today, while St. John is said to have taken the Virgin Mary to spend her last years in Ephesus. Whatever the truth of these legends, Anatolia was the staging ground of early Christian missionary activity, not only to the west but also to the east along the Silk Road.

For thousands of years, Anatolia had been an important thoroughfare for trade, but it reached new heights in A.D. 330, when Emperor Constantine, who had converted to Christianity, moved his capital from Rome to the ancient city of Byzantium. Renamed Constantinople, it became the grandest, most important city in the Roman world, perhaps the grandest and most important city in the entire world at that time. Now the Silk Road stretched the length of Anatolia to Constantinople, and the light of Greek and Roman culture continued to shine long after the fall of the Western Roman Empire in A.D. 476.

Turks, Islam, and the Great Seljuks

The Turks were a large group of tribes that originated in the high plateau of Mongolia and spread throughout much of Central Asia. In the sixth century a Chinese source described a great Turkish empire that stretched from the Great Wall in the East to the Black Sea in the West. At this time, the Turks lived north of the Silk Road but that soon changed as some tribes moved into present-day Uzbekistan and converted to Islam. By 1030, these Turks controlled lands from central Persia into northern India.

By this time, a new Turkish tribe migrated from the Steppes into northern Iran, where they too converted to Islam. Known as the Seljuks (1037-1194), after their first great "khan" or chieftain, they defeated their fellow Turks in Persia and took control of Baghdad in 1055. Later, the Seljuks invaded Georgia, and Armenia, before defeating the Byzantine army at Manzikert, in eastern Anatolia, in 1071. This was the beginning of the end for the once great Byzantine Empire. The Seljuks conquered most of Anatolia outside of Constantinople, with other Turkish tribes—some supporting the Seljuks and others hostile to them—controlling a number of smaller states.

At its height, in 1092, the Seljuk Empire stretched from the Hindu Kush Mountains along the modern Afghanistan-Pakistan border all the way to the Mediterranean, controlling the western half of the Silk Road. As a result, Turkish became the *lingua franca* of the Silk Road and even today elements of Turkish language can be understood in the spoken language from Istanbul to Xi'an in western China.

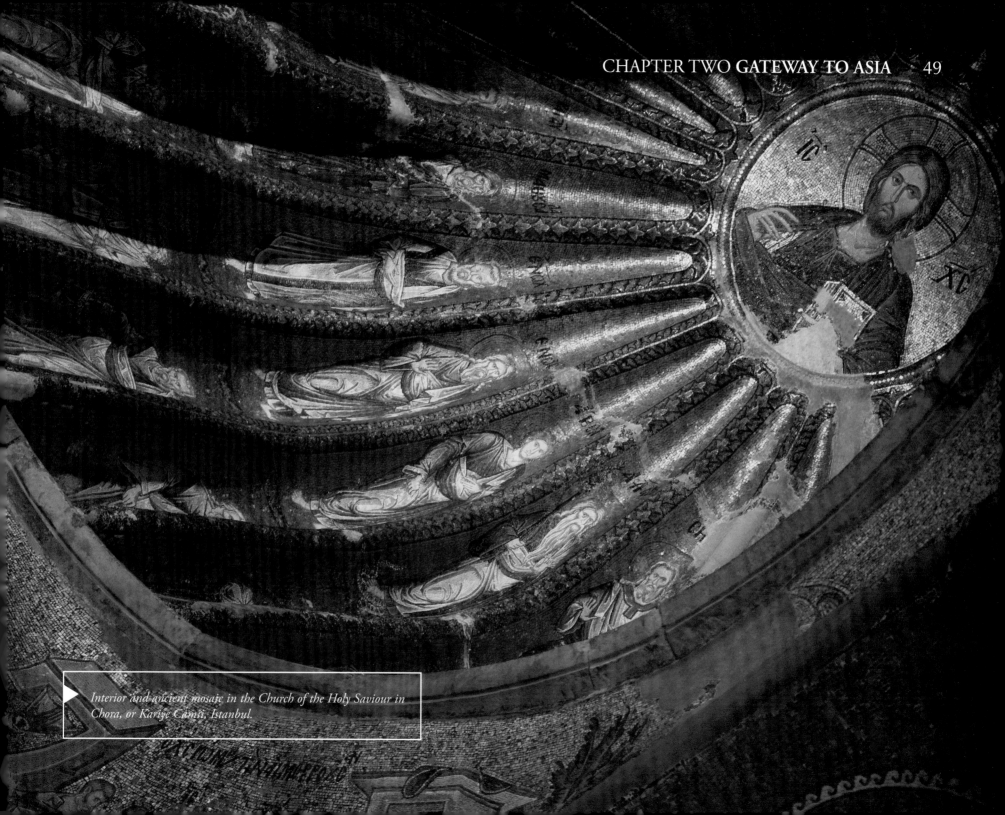

Interior and ancient mosaic in the Church of the Holy Saviour in Chora, or Kariye Camii, Istanbul.

Trade along the Silk Road brought great riches to the Seljuks. In order to protect and encourage this trade, they built almost 100 resting and trading stations, called caravanserais, where the caravans could stop for up to three days, with food, animal fodder, and lodging provided free of charge—courtesy of a wealthy Seljuk who endowed the caravanserai as a religious offering.

Although they came in a variety of different sizes and architectural designs, a typical Seljuk caravanserai was a large square or rectangular stone structure surrounding an open area for the camels, donkeys, horses, and other beasts of the caravan. It also housed human travellers outside during good weather. Although the walls were plain, the caravans entered through a grand archway elaborately decorated with geometric designs. Among the buildings that might be found inside was a grand hall to shelter the travellers and their goods in bad weather, a small mosque or prayer room, a kitchen, a treasury, a bath house, and repair shops. A number of small rooms were constructed around the courtyard where wealthier merchants could rest, protected from the noise and smells of the inner courtyard. Many Seljuk caravanserais can still be seen in Turkey and other countries along the Silk Road, and each visit effortlessly evokes once more the splendour and marvel of those ancient days.

The Crusades and the Mongols

The rise of the Seljuks and their threat to Constantinople prompted Byzantine Emperor Alexios I to appeal to Pope Urban II for a Christian army to help him drive back the Muslim Turks. Warriors of the First Crusade arrived outside Constantinople in the winter of 1096 and pushed into

An archway leads into the courtyard of an ancient caravanserai, the "hotel" and trading stop for many a merchant along the Silk Road. These buildings are found in all sorts of shapes and sizes throughout the route.

Anatolia, where they took the walled and lake-protected Seljuk capital of Nicaea (Iznik)—with help from boats that Emperor Alexios had rolled to them by land. Moving on to the south-east, they faced a longer and more difficult siege before conquering the great city of Antioch in June 1098. A year later, after another siege of barely a month, the Crusaders entered the holy city of Jerusalem.

The First Crusade, and those that followed, changed the political and cultural balance of the eastern Mediterranean world. The Crusaders established a number of "Crusader States" that gave western Europeans a foothold in Asia. Just as important was the fact that Latin Christians now travelled the Silk Road along with Greek-speaking Eastern Christians, Muslims, Jews and Armenians. For the Europeans, the journey into the Islamic world brought a rediscovery of classical Roman scholarship, which had been kept alive by Islamic scholars even as it had faded in the west.

The next two centuries saw a chaotic mix of cultures and political forces in Anatolia. In the 1140s, The Seljuks won back much of the lands they had lost to the Crusaders, but the real threat to the Byzantine Empire came from within the Christian world. Between 1204 and 1261, a multitude of Europeans claimed the title of emperor in what was called the Latin Empire of Byzantium. By the time the Greek empire was re-established, all that was left of it in Asia was a foothold in western Anatolia.

The great Asian power of this time was the Mongol Empire, which at its height in 1279 stretched from Korea into eastern Europe and controlled almost every kilometre of the main thoroughfares of the Silk

Pottery designs, at a market in the Grand Bazaar in Istanbul, reflect the influences of two thousand years of Silk Road history.

Road. Twenty years earlier, in 1259, the Seljuks joined the Mongols and attacked Damascus in return for the right to retain rule over Anatolia as a vassal state. By the 1330s, however, Mongol power was broken and a new power began to emerge: the Ottoman Turks.

The Ottomans

As the Seljuk Empire faded, small Turkish states called emirates, or *beyliks*, struggled for power in Anatolia. From this period of conflict, the Ottomans emerged as a major military force. In 1354, they crossed the Dardanelles—where Alexander had crossed some 1700 years earlier—and established the beginning of an empire in south-eastern Europe. By 1367, with the exception of its outlet on the Bosporus Strait, Constantinople was completely surrounded, an island of Greek Christianity in a sea of Turkish Islam.

The Ottomans were temporarily stopped near the ancient city of Ankara in 1402 by the Central Asian leader Timur (Tamerlane), who dreamt of re-establishing the Mongol Empire and regaining control over the Silk Road from China to Constantinople. Although a formidable leader, Timur was by then an old man and his dream died with him just three years later. After the Mongols withdrew, the Ottomans continued their expansion westward into Europe and eastward into Asia.

In 1453, the Ottomans conquered Constantinople, which would later be renamed Istanbul, from the Greek phrase *eis tin polin*, "to the city." As the Ottomans continued to expand their empire throughout eastern Europe, western Asia, and northern Africa, they controlled trade in the eastern Mediterranean, the Aegean Sea, the Black Sea, and the Red Sea. They also controlled much of the western Silk Road, but the road was no longer the great trans-Asian trade route it once was by the time they ascended to power.

End of the Road

Scholars point to the breakup of the Mongol Empire in early 1300s as the beginning of the end of the Silk Road. By around 1400, as ships became stronger and the Silk Road became more dangerous and expensive, silk no longer reached the west over the ancient land route, carried instead by water on the old Spice Routes through the Indian Ocean and into the Red Sea. Although the overland trading routes continued to be important to the regional economies, they never regained their former glory.

The conquest of Constantinople half a century later was perhaps the symbolic end of this era. From the European point of view, the entire land route through Asia to China was now controlled by Muslims who would charge the steepest prices they could to allow traders to pass through their lands—if they allowed them to pass at all. The Spice Routes were not ideal, either, because pirates still roamed the seas and the Red Sea ports were controlled by Arabs, Egyptians, and later the Ottoman Turks. For Europe, the answer was to find direct sea routes to the East, and a new age of exploration began.

Left: The Hagia Sofia in Istanbul was declared a mosque in 1453 after Sultan Mehmet II allowed his troops to pillage and loot the city (then Constantinople). Trapped worshippers were killed and raped before an Islamic scholar took to the church's pulpit and recited out the Shahada - "There is no God but Allah, and Mohammed is His prophet".

Top and Bottom Right: The pomegranate may be an unlikely icon of the Silk Road, but, having originated in Iran, it travelled along the Silk Road trading routes into Central Asia, China and India. Greatly appreciated as a delicacy and important medicinal remedy, it also had symbolism in Christianity, Zoroastrianism, Jewish and Islamic religions.

Persian Majolica tile work is ubiquitous in Iran's historical monuments. Since 1200 A.D., the Persians discovered how to create tiles with multiple colours that they used to decorate in mosaic styles.

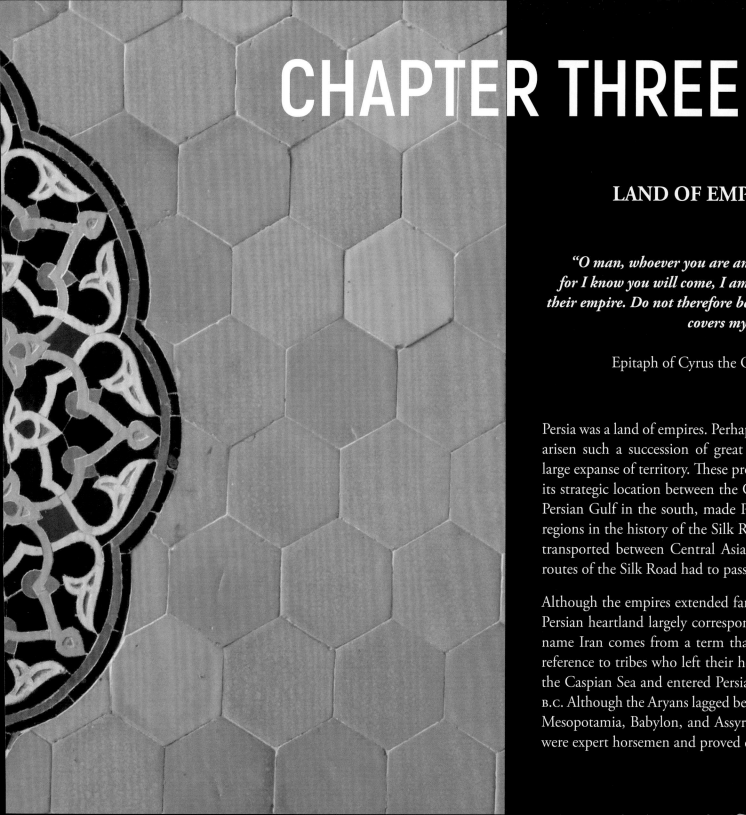

CHAPTER THREE

LAND OF EMPIRES: PERSIA

*"O man, whoever you are and wherever you come from,
for I know you will come, I am Cyrus who won the Persians
their empire. Do not therefore begrudge me this bit of earth that
covers my bones."*

Epitaph of Cyrus the Great c.600 - 530 B.C.

Persia was a land of empires. Perhaps nowhere in the world has there arisen such a succession of great empires that dominated such a large expanse of territory. These prominent empires, combined with its strategic location between the Caspian Sea in the north and the Persian Gulf in the south, made Persia one of the most significant regions in the history of the Silk Road. Put simply, any trade goods transported between Central Asia and Western Asia on the main routes of the Silk Road had to pass through Persia.

Although the empires extended far beyond its modern borders, the Persian heartland largely corresponded with present-day Iran. The name Iran comes from a term that means "land of the Aryans," a reference to tribes who left their homeland on the steppes north of the Caspian Sea and entered Persia early in the second millennium B.C. Although the Aryans lagged behind the sophisticated cultures of Mesopotamia, Babylon, and Assyria (all in modern-day Iraq), they were expert horsemen and proved devastating in battle.

In the late eighth century B.C. an Aryan group called the Medes consolidated territory in what is now north-western Iran and built a beautiful capital at Ecbatana (now called Hamedan), which would later became an important junction on the Silk Road. In 606 B.C. the Medes and Babylonians formed an alliance to defeat the powerful Assyrians, and the Medean Empire extended from Iran into Anatolia (Turkey). The rule of the Medes would not last long, however, for a new Aryan people, the Persians, would soon take over the throne.

The Persian Empire

The Persians were a group of tribes who settled in southern Iran, in the modern province of Fars. While they began to carve out their own small empire, they were dominated by the Medes until the rise of an inspirational king who became known as Cyrus the Great. Uniting the Persians behind him, Cyrus occupied the Medean capital of Ecbatana in 550 B.C. Three years later he conquered Anatolia in the west, and for the next six years drove east as far as Pakistan and Afghanistan. Finally, he returned to the west and conquered Babylon—where he freed the Jews from a half-century of captivity.

Cyrus was not only a great conqueror but also a great leader who tolerated other religions and cultures and treated his subjects with such fairness that, according to the Greek historian Xenophon, "he was able to awaken in them so lively a desire to please him, that they always wished to be guided by his will."

After Cyrus's death in 530 B.C., his son expanded the empire into Egypt but lost control of other regions leaving the new empire on the verge of collapse. Then, in 521 B.C., a young relative of Cyrus took the throne and ruled with such strength and vision that he would later be called Darius the Great.

Darius reorganized the political structure, dividing the empire into 20 provinces (*satraps*), each with a governor, a general, and a secretary of state. These officials reported directly to the central government and were rotated throughout the empire to keep them from getting too powerful. To further maintain honesty and good government, inspectors travelled from *satrap* to *satrap* listening to complaints and reporting back to the central government.

In order to keep this enlightened and sophisticated political structure functioning, Darius built an impressive network of roads throughout the empire, including the Royal Road[1] from his capital at Susa in the province of Fars to the city of Sardis near the Aegean Sea in western Anatolia. Soldiers patrolled the route to keep travellers safe, and fast-riding messengers provided a personal communication service for Darius.

The main route from Susa merged at Arbela (present day Arbil in northern Iraq) onto the Silk Road towards the west while a spur led to Ecbatana and further on towards the east. To collect taxes and further stimulate trade, Darius introduced a system of gold and silver coins and standard weights and measures. Although silk did not yet travel along the road—and the East remained shrouded in mystery—a steady stream of goods were carried through Persia, from luxury items and precious metals to common household goods, clothing, and grain. The western half of the Silk Road and the many routes that fed it were open for business, and Darius needed to be able to centralise and unify trade as it entered and travelled through his empire.

---

1   *The Royal Road was an ancient highway that Darius rebuilt and reconnected during the fifth century B.C. primarily to facilitate rapid communication throughout his Persian Empire.*

A relief at the ancient Imperial Palace of Persepolis, in Iran, depicting the head of a Persian solider. UNESCO declared the ruins of Persepolis a World Heritage Site in 1979.

Zoroastrianism

The enlightened rule of Cyrus and Darius reflected the teachings of Zoroastrianism, a religion with such enigmatic roots that most scholars believe that it was established in ancient Iran long before the time of Cyrus - probably its beginnings date from many centuries earlier. According to Zoroastrian scriptures, its founder, Zarathustra (Zoroaster in Greek), set out across the Iranian Plateau preaching a new theology of one God, Ahura Mazda the Creator, and an equal force of evil, Ahriman the Destroyer. Some linguists interpret the name Zarathustra as meaning "golden camel," an intriguing image for a mystical prophet of the Silk Road crossing a desert landscape.

Zoroastrianism and Judaism were the world's first monotheistic religions, and there are many similarities between the two—not surprising considering that Jews lived near Persia during the Babylonia exile and that Judea later became a Persian province. The Silk Road allowed both Zoroastrianism and Judaism to travel eastwards into Asia with relative ease, as it would also serve as a conduit for Buddhism, Christianity, and Islam. Religious beliefs developed along the Silk Road much like natural organisms – growing and adapting to their surrounding environment, splitting off as they mature and occasionally dying, leaving an indelible mark upon civilisation. Zoroastrianism was just the start of a new branch of monotheistic religions that we have come to know ever since.

That Zoroastrian beliefs look and feel familiar today, as they emphasize social justice, good works, and good deeds, is the most basic proof of the Silk Road's heritage. Zoroastrians believe the purpose of mankind's battle on the side of good against evil is the betterment of society. Many later religions still contain portions of Zoroastrian beliefs, most strikingly perhaps in their modern-day rites and rituals – a Christian baptism uses symolism of fire and water in similar ways to the Zoroastrian purification

The ruins of the ancient city of Persepolis, Iran, once the ceremonial capital of the Achaemenid Empire (c. 550-330 B.C.). Chosen by Cyrus the Great, it was Darius I who built the terraces and palaces.

rituals – fire gives spiritual insight while water gives wisdom. So powerful was this religion in Persia that in a famous inscription on Darius' tomb, the dead king speaks:

"By the desire of Ahura Mazda this is my nature: to that which is just I am a friend, to that which is unjust I am no friend. I do not wish that the weak should suffer harm at the hands of the powerful, nor that the powerful should suffer harm at the hands of the weak. Whatever is just, that is my desire."

The Greek Interlude

The Persian Empire fell in the face of Alexander the Great's onslaught through Asia. After destroying the Persian army of Darius III near Syria in 333 B.C., Alexander finished his conquest two years later at the Battle of Arbela, thought to have taken place near Mosul in modern Iraq.

While Darius fled to the east, travelling along the Silk Road, Alexander marched south through the great cities of the empire. He was received as a liberator in Babylon, just as Cyrus had been received two centuries earlier. He subsequently occupied the two great Persian capitals: Susa and Persepolis, and plundered their vast wealth.

Persepolis, which had been established by Darius the Great, was one of the most beautiful cities in the world. Using 10,000 horses and 5,000 camels, Alexander looted the city of its precious jewels, 120,000 talents of silver, and 8,000 talents of gold, worth billions of dollars in today's value. Then, in an event that still puzzles historians—who view Alexander as an enlightened ruler who appreciated beauty—the city was burned to the ground.

Ruins of the Gate of All Nations in Persepolis, Iran, viewed from the side. The construction was ordered by Achaemenid king Xerxes I (486-465 B.C.).

Leaving the ashes of Persepolis behind, Alexander marched north to loot the former Medean capital of Ecbatana. He headed east on the Silk Road, though the Caspian Gates—a mountain pass east of present-day Tehran—and continued on the Silk Road to conquer the furthest reaches of the Persian empire. While Greek culture influenced all the lands he conquered, Alexander himself was also greatly influenced by Persian culture. He adopted the purple robes of Persian kings—which disturbed his Greek soldiers, who felt their leader was losing the spirit of equality among comrades in arms.

After Alexander died in Babylon in 323 B.C., his vast eastern conquests, including Persia, were ruled by the Greek dynasty called the Seleucids, founded by Seleucus Nicator, who emerged with the largest prize among Alexander's generals. Although Greek culture dominated in Syria and Anatolia to the west, it never fully took hold in Persia. The ruling class spoke Greek and adopted Greek ways in order to maintain their power, but the common people remained Persian in their hearts and minds. It is an interesting parallel to note how Central Asia has emerged from decades of Soviet rule and today looks back to its ancient Silk Road traditions.

The Parthians

The Parthians were yet another nomadic Aryan tribe that migrated from north of the Caspian Sea and settled in eastern Iran. Gradually gaining strength, they seized control of Persia by 163 B.C., cutting if off from the Seleucid Empire to the west. Though not Persian ethnically, they brought a return to Persian culture after the Greeks.

It was during Parthian rule that the Silk Road opened from the east. Around 106 B.C., the Chinese—who had recently conquered the strategic city of Khokand in present-day Uzbekistan—sent a mission all the way to Persia where they were received with great honours, as described two centuries later in *The Annals of the Former Han Dynasty*:

Constructed in around 575 B.C., under the orders of King Nebuchadnezzar II, the Ishtar Gate was the eight gateway to the inner city of Babylon. Following a twentieth century excavation, it now appears in reconstructed and restored form in Berlin's Pergamon museum.

The sovereign ordered his military chiefs to meet the Chinese ambassa-
dor at the eastern frontier with 20,000 horsemen—and from the fron-
tier to the capital [Hecatompylos] there is a distance of several thousand
li. The road passed through some dozens of towns. The population covers
the land almost without a break."

A "li" at this time equalled about 415 metres, so the escort met the ambassador far from the Parthian capital, well into Central Asia, and the
Silk Road was already well populated.

This was, perhaps, the moment that gave birth to the Silk Road as a
continuous route across Asia. For the next eight centuries the Persians
and Chinese would be allies, controlling trade between East and West.
On this first meeting of the two cultures, the Persians were interested in
silk and other eastern luxuries, while the Chinese were fascinated with
ostriches, tumblers, and jugglers. It is probable that these items were
themselves brought to Persia from Egypt.

According to the *Annals*: "When the Chinese mission left, the sovereign…sent with them an ambassador of his own that he might learn
something of China. To the Chinese court he presented an ostrich egg
and some conjurors from Li-Kan. The son of Heaven took great pleas-
ure in these."

The identity of Li-Kan is uncertain. Some scholars think it refers to
Alexandria, Egypt, which was famous for performers; others think it
refers to the Greek trading town of Petra in Jordan. For the Chinese, it
signified the world beyond Parthia, and from this time, they began to
reach towards that world, not yet knowing it was the Roman Empire.

The large prayer hall in the Masjid-i-Vakil (Vakil Mosque) is some
75 metres long and 36 metres wide, housing some of the most intri-
cate twisted columns cut out of one single block of stone. Constructed
in 1773 it is found in Shiraz, Iran.

The Sassanid Empire

The Parthians ruled until A.D. 224, valiantly holding off the Romans on the West and protecting their eastern frontier from Central Asian tribes—keeping a long stretch of the Silk Road open in the process. Although they were great warriors, they struggled to remain united and fell to the Persian Sassanids, who ushered in a golden age of Persian culture that lasted until the Islamic invasion.

The rise of the Sassanids corresponded with the fall of the Han Dynasty in China and the decline of the Roman Empire. Expanding their empire from Mesopotamia in the west to the Pamir Mountains in the east, these Persians were the superpower of Eurasia, by far the strongest nation on the Silk Road. They carefully protected their position, controlling the flow of goods both on the Silk Road and the Spice Route. The latter route was achieved by holding the seaports of Mesopotamia where spices reached the west. In time, Persian ships would eventually sail all the way to China, trading for silk and spices directly at the port of Canton (today a sprawling Chinese city called Guangzhou).

After the fall of the Roman Empire, the Sassanids battled the Byzantine Empire, which had developed a voracious appetite for silk, both for the wealthy class and for the Eastern Orthodox Church. One of the key areas of conflict was the southern Caucasus region of present-day Armenia, Georgia, and Azerbajian. For the Byzantines, the western Caucasus provided access from the Black Sea to a route across the steppes and into Central Asia that allowed them to bypass the Persians. Another northern route, along the western coast of the Caspian Sea in modern Azerbaijian, connected directly with the main Silk Road at the Persian crossroads city of Rey (just south of modern Tehran).

During the Sassanid period, Persian silk textiles, including exquisite carpets, were in demand along the Silk Road from China to western Europe.

The splendid colours in the Masjid-i-Vakil are an assault on the senses as exquisite mosaic tiles cover the ceiling.

The Persians also became known for beautiful gilded silver objects such as flasks, bowls, and plates. Both of these technologies were exported on the Silk Road to other cultures; aided by Persian experts, artisans in Tang China began producing beautiful silverware with Chinese motifs. Sassanid coins, along with silk yarn and plain silk textiles, became standard currency on the Silk Road. The Persians also introduced bills of exchange, predecessors of modern cheques, which later became the basis of the banking system of the Italian Renaissance.

Ironically, the Sassanid Empire began to collapse just as it reached its height. In the early seventh century A.D., after the Sassanids conquered Syria, Jerusalem, and Alexandria, and threatened Constantinople, the Byzantine Emperor Heraclius regained much of the lost territory and drove them back into Persia. By this time, both empires were exhausted from near-constant warfare and became easy prey for a new power that came from the south.

The Islamic Caliphates

The Arab armies conquered Persia with amazing speed. In 636, just four years after the death of the prophet Muhammad, they won a decisive victory at al-Qadisiyyah in present-day Iraq and went on to take nearby Ctesiphon, a great Silk Road city that was the winter capital of both the Parthians and Sassanians. Today the ruins lie approximately 35 kilometres south of present-day Baghdad. In 641, another victory near Ecbatana sent the last Sassanian monarch on the run, and the Arabs overwhelmed the rest of the empire province by province. By 651 the conquest was complete.

Beginning in 661, Persia was ruled from Damascus, Syria, by the Caliphs (successors to the Prophet) of the Umayyid Dyasty, with Arab governors ruling local regions. Unlike many cultures conquered by the Arabs, the Persians held onto their language and identity while gradually converting to Islam.

The octagonal Kajeh Rabi' Tomb, just north of Mashhad, Iran.

Persian culture was further strengthened in 776, when a new dynasty of Caliphs, the Abbasids, moved their capital to Baghdad—a new city built by the Abbasids just 30 kilometres from the old Persian capital of Ctesiphon and in a region long dominated by Persian influence. The Abbasid Caliphate has been called the Golden Age of Islam, and Persians were a driving force behind its greatness. An Abbasid Caliph is recorded as saying, "The Persians ruled for a thousand years and did not need us Arabs even for a day. We have been ruling them for one or two centuries and cannot do without them for an hour."

As Islam spread throughout Asia, the Silk Road fell firmly under Islamic control. It was during this period that paper manufacture passed from China to the west; the first paper mill was built in Baghdad during the reign of Caliph Harun al-Rashid (786-809).

The Seljuks

The Umayyid Caliphate began to collapse during the ninth century A.D. and a series of dynasties fought for control of what had once been the eastern Persian Empire, often called Greater Khorasan (containing parts of Iran, Afghanistan, Turkmenistan, Uzbekistan, and Tajikistan), and ultimately the heart of Persia. Inevitably, none of these local dynasties could hold onto power for long. In the early eleventh century, Turkish tribesmen called the Seljuks (1037-1194) emerged from this period of dynastic conflict as a new force.

Originally from the Central Asian steppes, the Seljuks moved south into Greater Khorasan in the late tenth century and adopted Islam. In 1037, under their "Great Seljuk," Toghril Beg, they marched toward the west along the Silk Road, peacefully taking the great trading cities of Merv in modern Turkmenistan and Nishapur in eastern Iran. They continued driving westward on the Road, taking Rey and Hamadan (the former Medean capital of Ecbatana) in 1044. By 1060, Toghril Beg had established Seljuk rule throughout Persia.

The Seljuks brought a new period of stability to Persia, allowing trade to flourish on the Silk Road and other connecting routes. Art, literature and science also prospered and theological schools sprang up across the empire propagating the Sunni branch of Islam (today, however, it is the Shia branch that dominates). Their last great leader, Malik-Shah (who ruled from 1072-1092) made his capital at the ancient city of Esfahan in central Iran, on a trade route that ran southward from Rey, through Esfahan, on to Shiraz (near the ancient capital of Persepolis) and across the Persian Gulf to Mecca. Rey was also the northern terminus of another important north-south trading route through the desert cities of Yazd and Kerman to the Red Sea port of Hormuz.

After the death of Malik-Shah in 1092, the Seljuk Empire fell apart due to conflicting claims of leadership. The decline was hastened by religious warriors called Ismailis—whom Europeans named the Assassins (from hashashin, meaning "hash users," based on an unsubstantiated belief that they were given hashish to smoke in order to experience the paradise they would enter if they were courageous in battle). Basing their operations in inaccessible castles throughout Persia, most notably the supposedly impregnable castle of Alamut in the mountains north of Tehran, the Assassins maintained steady pressure on the Seljuks. In time, however, a new force would sweep through Persia that was too strong for the Seljuks or the Assassins.

▶ *A tower of silence stands tall in Yazd, Iran. Atop these forma-
tions, the Zoroastrian dead are left to the birds leaving only
their bones to bury in special clay ossuaries.*

The Mongols and Tamerlane

In 1220 a massive army of Mongol warriors under Tolui, the son of Genghis Khan, rode west on the Silk Road and attacked the eastern Persian cities of Merv and Nishapur, at that time two of the largest cities of the world. The Mongols burned the cities to the ground and killed all their inhabitants. In Nishapur, they beheaded every citizen, separated the heads among men, women, and children, and stacked them into neat pyramids, throwing the carcasses of dogs and cats around them. Then they disembowelled the headless bodies. According to one story, this extraordinary brutality was ordered by the daughter of Genghis Khan after her husband was killed in the city.

The Mongols overran much of Persia, not only leaving death in their wake but also destroying the lifeblood of the people: the ingenious underground irrigation systems called *qanats* that enabled the Persians to live an agricultural life in a desert land by tapping into aquifers underground. Dating back to before the time of Cyrus the Great, *qanat* technology spread throughout the sphere of Persian influence. The same technology, once transferred along the Silk Road, is still found today in the Chinese oases of the Taklamakan desert, the Arabian peninsula and in North Africa. In Iran, however, it would take many generations for the land to recover.

Persia faced a second wave of Mongol destruction between 1256 and 1258 A.D., when Genghis Khan's grandson, Hulagu, again ravaged northern Iran on his way to Baghdad, where he captured the last Abassid Caliph and had him placed in a sack and kicked to death by horses. Along the way, the once-feared Assassins surrendered their inaccessible castle of Alamut without a fight.

The Azadi Tower is one of the dominating landmarks in Tehran, marking the western entrance to the modern city.

Hulagu and his descendants established a new dynasty in Persia called the Il-khanate, with their capital at Maragheh in modern Azerbaijan and later at Tabriz in north-western Iran. Owing allegiance to the Great Khan (his brother Möngke Khan) in China, they further strengthened the connections between Persia and China while continuing to open relations with western Europe. Despite its violent beginnings, some of the greatest Persian writers, scientists, and philosophers thrived under the Il-khanate dynasty. The Mongol domination had brought an era of peace and prosperity to the Silk Road.

Around 1295 A.D., toward the end of his homeward journey, Marco Polo, his father, and his uncle stopped in Tabriz to deliver a Mongolian princess to her husband. "The men get their living by trade and handicrafts," he wrote, "for they weave many kinds of beautiful and valuable stuffs of silk and gold. The city has such a good position that merchandise is brought thither from India, Badua [Baghdad]...and many other regions; and that attracts many Latin merchants, especially Genoese, to buy goods and transact other business there; the more as it is also a great market for precious stones. It is a city in fact where merchants make large profits."

The Il-khanate dynasty ended in 1335 A.D. and for half a century, petty nobles fought for control of the empire. Into this atmosphere of chaos swept one last scourge from the east: the Tatar warlord Tamerlane, who raided the former Persian Empire between 1381 and 1402, leaving death and destruction in his wake. Unlike the Mongols, he did not stop to govern but rather focused on looting artistic treasures and human talents and taking them back to his own capital of Samarkand in the east. By the time he was gone, the glories of the Silk Road were coming to an end and Persia faced a long road to recovery. Although, from the splinters of the Timurid realm, one final dynasty, the Safavids (1501-1736), tried to restore the glories of yesteryear and did bring some level of prosperity to cities such as Esfahan under Shah Abbas I (1588-1629), the connections with the Silk Road never flourished in the same way again.

An elderly lady sports the traditional costume of the small village of Abyaneh in Esfahan province in Iran. Dating back 1,500 years, the colourful floral hijab distinguishes women from other parts of Iran that sport plain hijabs or full-length black chadors.

An Uzbek bride patiently awaits her husband-to-be at home. Before the marriage a **mullah** will ask her marital consent and read a prayer ('nikokh'), which effects the marriage.

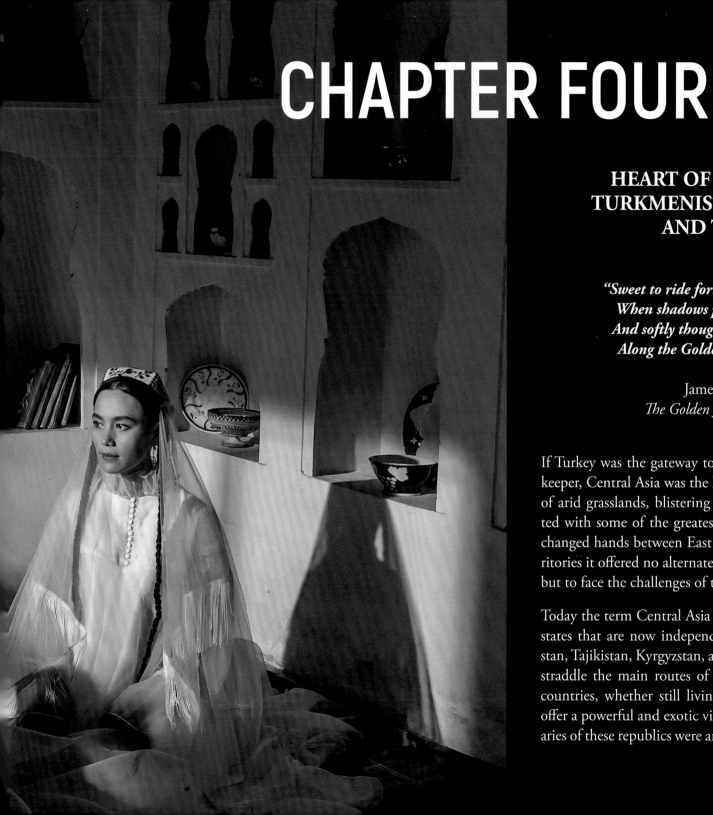

CHAPTER FOUR

HEART OF THE SILK ROAD: TURKMENISTAN, UZBEKISTAN, AND TAJIKISTAN

"Sweet to ride forth at evening from the wells
When shadows pass gigantic on the sand,
And softly though the silence beat the bells
Along the Golden Road to Samarkand."

James Elroy Flecker
The Golden Journey to Samarkand

If Turkey was the gateway to Europe and Persia the powerful gate-keeper, Central Asia was the heart of the Silk Road, a rugged region of arid grasslands, blistering deserts, and towering mountains dotted with some of the greatest trading cities where goods and ideas changed hands between East and West. Unlike other Silk Road territories it offered no alternate routes by sea, so traders had no choice but to face the challenges of the land.

Today the term Central Asia is usually applied to five former Soviet states that are now independent republics: Turkmenistan, Uzbekistan, Tajikistan, Kyrgyzstan, and Kazakhstan. Of these, the first three straddle the main routes of the Silk Road and the cities in these countries, whether still living or preserved in archaeological sites, offer a powerful and exotic view of past glories. The modern boundaries of these republics were artificially created by Soviet ruler, Joseph

Stalin, between 1924 and 1936 in an effort to limit the political power of the people who lived in the region, most of whom shared Turkic origins and Islamic beliefs. Before Stalin, it was known as Turkestan, but over the centuries various areas have been known by different names with their true boundaries defined more by deserts, rivers, and mountains than politics.

For the history of the Silk Road in this region, the most important geographic feature was the Pamir Mountains, situated in modern Tajikistan, the great barrier and dividing line between China and Central Asia, and still a part of China's western border. Another important feature was the Amu Darya, a river that flows from the Pamirs towards the Aral and Caspian seas and forms part of the modern boundary between Uzbekistan and Turkmenistan. Called the Oxus by the Greeks, the river, along with the Syr Darya or Jaxartes River, defined a region called Transoxiana, literally "beyond the Oxus."

Persians, Greeks, and Arabs all projected their power into Central Asia from the west, while the Turks and Mongols established their power in the region before their further westward invasions. Thus, much of its Silk Road history unfolds within the framework of these empires. Yet the region also fostered local empires that controlled large and strategic sections of the Silk Road. They were a resourceful people who became the Silk Road's greatest traders, and built a network of exotic cities that came to define the Silk Road.

Bactria and Sogdiana

Bactria and Sogdiana were the two most eastern *satrapies* (provinces) of the Persian Empire. Located in present-day northern Afghanistan between the Hindu Kush Mountains and the Amu Darya, the heart of Bactria was a fertile plain watered by the mountain streams. Some 4,000 years ago, an advanced farming culture developed in this area and the

An exquisitely carved wooden door at the tomb of Naqshbandi near Bukhara. Baha-ud-Din Naqshband founded one of the largest Sufi Muslim orders, the Naqshbandi.

adjacent region of Margiana in modern Turkmenistan. The people of this culture may have been the same Aryan tribes who later migrated into Persia and India.

Bactria gave its name to the two-humped Bactrian camel, which was domesticated in the region around 2500 B.C., well before the arrival of the Persians. Stockier, furrier, and hardier than the one-humped dromedary from Arabia, the Bactrian camel became an indispensable beast of burden in caravan trade on the Silk Road. Along with its great endurance in the desert extremes of searing heat and freezing cold, it could also sense the proximity of water better than people and could forewarn of an approaching sandstorm. Without this animal, many more travellers would have perished attempting to cross Central Asia's deserts and the Silk Road may never have developed to quite the same extent.

Sogdiana was located in south-eastern Uzbekistan and western Tajikistan, centred in the valley of the Zarafshan River. The Sogdians were tough, independent warriors who formed a buffer zone between the Persian Empire and the nomadic tribes of the steppes. Later, they became the greatest traders on the Silk Road, dominating the route from the Karakum desert of Turkmenistan to the end of the road in China.

Some scholars believe that Zoroaster was born in Bactria and began his ministry there, rather than in the mountains of north-western Iran. The Sogdians also claim him as a native son. Whatever its origins, Zoroastrianism took firm hold in both Bactria and Sogdiana. When Alexander the Great occupied the region in 329-327 B.C., his disregard of Zoroastrian religious beliefs sparked a rebellion led by the *satrap* (governor) of Sogdiana with Bactrian support. In putting down the rebellion, Alexander's army conquered a mountain stronghold called the Sogdian Rock, near the Sogdian capital of Samarkand. Among the prisoners of war was a beautiful Bactrian noblewoman named Roxanne, whom Alexander married, thereby cementing his hold over the far eastern provinces.

A traditional Central Asian offering of nuts and dried fruits that will often be brought out on a whim upon the arrival of a visitor.

Alexander combined Bactria and Sogdiana into a single *satrap* and, as he did throughout his empire, built a Greek city beside the Bactrian capital of Bactra leaving a colony of Greeks behind. Thus Greek culture continued to develop in this distant region, the furthest eastern reach of Hellenisation. Around 250 B.C., at the time the Parthians were shaking off the Greek yoke in Persia, an independent Greco-Bactrian state maintained its hold over Bactria and Sogdiana, ruling for about 125 years until nomadic horsemen, called the Yuezhi, pushed them south into India.

The Kushan Empire and Buddhism

The Yuezhi were a confederacy of Indo-European people from the arid grasslands of the Tarim Basin in what is now western China. Around 175 B.C. they were pushed westward by a larger confederacy called the Xiongnu. Some 20 years later, they were forced to move again and settled on the northern bank of the Amu Darya. Between 129 and 127 B.C., a Chinese envoy named Zhang Qian visited the Yuezhi and reported, "They are a nation of nomads, moving from place to place with their herds... They have some 100,000 or 200,000 archer warriors."

Not long after Zhang Qian's visit, the Yuezhi conquered Bactria and synthesized Greek and Bactrian culture with their own, gradually transitioning from a nomadic to sedentary way of life. Sometime before A.D. 100, one of the five Yuezhi tribes, the Guishuang, established dominance and formed a new realm that became known as the Kushan Empire. The Kushan people expanded deep into India, where many of them converted to Buddhism.

With control of Indian ports and trade routes, as well as the network of east-west routes through Bactria and Sogdiana, the Kushans became—along with the Roman, Persian, and Chinese empires—one of the great

The mesmerising geometric shapes from a hallway in a mosque in Shakhrisabz, Uzbekistan.

powers of the Silk Road. This was a period of vibrant travel, when the Silk Road was open from China to Byzantium, and the Kushans, who at their height controlled the route from Persia into present-day western China, occupied a strategic location of extraordinary cultural interaction.

Their greatest contribution was to disseminate Buddhism throughout their own territory and along the Silk Road to China. Buddhist cave shrines and monasteries became regular features on the eastern half of the Silk Road, offering shelter and a place to worship. The Kushans also took Buddhism to Persia, and although it never became a powerful religion there, Persian Buddhists joined Kushans and Indians as missionaries to the east. Buddhism paved the way for the transmittal of other religions from Persia to China, including Nestorian Christianity and an offshoot of Zoroastrianism called Manichaeism.

The role of the Kushans and the great wealth generated by trade changed Buddhism itself, developing a new form, called Mahayana (Great Vehicle), designed to appeal to merchants and non-Indians. Buddha was transformed from a simple sage to a more godlike figure, and while wealthy merchants could not relate to traditional Buddhist austerity, they could embrace the idea that giving generously of their wealth would earn them spiritual returns. Buddhist monasteries became repositories of enormous wealth and exquisite art, funded in large part by the merchants of the Silk Road. Although some of the most striking extant sites are in China, the remains of Kushan temples and monasteries have been found in the Termez area of southern Uzbekistan at Kara Tepe, Fayaz Tepe, and Dalverzin Tepe.

Traditional Uzbek locksmith in Andijan.

The Great Trading Cities

The Kushan Empire collapsed over the course of a century, after the death of its last great leader, Vasudeva I (A.D. 190-225) whereupon the empire split into western and eastern halves that would soon be subjugated by others. New empires would rise and fall, but regardless of their rulers, many of the great trading cities continued to prosper as wealthy market-places. Most of these cities were located in desert oases, offering life-giving water in an arid land and providing travelling merchant caravans natural and critical staging posts for trade and recuperation. Their names have been immortalised in legends that describe their splendour and majesty.

Ashgabat, Konjikala, and Nisa (Turkmenistan)

The capital of Turkmenistan, Ashgabat, is often called the "City of Love" based on an interpretation of its name in modern Persian. Located in the Akhal Oasis near the northern border of Iran, on the edge of the desert it is buffered by the Kopet-Dag mountains providing a sprawling backdrop to the city. Ashgabat grew from a small village on top the ruins of Konjikala, once an important Silk Road city first mentioned as a notable wine producing centre in the second century B.C. Konjikala was completely destroyed by an earthquake in the late first century B.C. but was rebuilt and continued to thrive until destroyed again in the Mongol invasion. Today Ashgabat owes its revival to the Russian Empire, who developed the city to ensure it had accessible proximity to British-influenced Persia in the nineteenth century. The modern cityscape of Ashgabat has been sculpted largely by Turkmenistan's first president, Saparmurat Niyazov, following its independence from the Soviet Union in 1991. He created a Disney-like atmosphere of overly grand monumental buildings, palaces, theatres, sporting arenas and mosques to herald the glory of independent Turkmenistan.

Old men don't answer, they just tell stories: A weathered Uzbek farmer pensively surveys his crops in Termez.

About 18 km to the northwest of Ashgabat are the ruins of Nisa, an ancient city believed to have been a Parthian capital and the burial place of Parthian kings. Archaeological evidence indicates that it was once an important and wealthy city with impressive public buildings, mausoleums, and Greek-inspired artwork. Nisa was destroyed in the same earthquake that flattened Konjikala, but unlike Konjikala it was never rebuilt.

Watered by streams from the Kopet Dag Mountains along the modern border between Turkmenistan and Iran, the Akhal Oasis is home to the famous Akhal-Teke horses, reknowned for their speed, stamina, comfortable gaits, intelligence, and trainability. Considered one of the world's oldest horse breeds—and still highly valued today—they are perfectly suited for their native desert environment and were prized by those who had the good fortune to ride them on the Silk Road. These magnificent horses are one of Turkmenistan's national emblems appearing in the national flag slong with carpet symbolism and sheaves of wheat.

Merv (Turkmenistan)

More than 80% of Turkmenistan is covered by the Karakum Desert, which formed a natural barrier between Persia to the west and Transoxiana to the east. Although there were multiple Silk Road routes on either side of the desert, nearly all routes led to the great oasis city of Merv. For travellers from the west, Merv was the "Gateway to Central Asia" while for those from the east it was the entrance to Persia.

Merv owed its importance to the Murghab River, which rises in central Afghanistan and flows north into Turkmenistan where it forms a delta and disappears into the desert. Merv was not a single city, but rather a series of four walled urban settlements on the river banks that today lie in ruins near modern Bayram-Ali about 30 km east of the modern city of Mary. Although already significant under the Persian and Greek empires, Merv blossomed under the Parthians and Sassanians during the first six

The "Eternal Glory" monument in the town of Mary, southern Turkmenistan. Lying in the delta of the Murghab river, the city is surrounded by the sands of the Karakum desert, thirty kilometres away from the ancient city of Merv.

centuries A.D., when it had its own mint and issued its own coins. It was not only a trading centre, but a meeting place of world religions: Zoroastrianism Manichaeism, Judaism, Buddhism, and Christianity.

The city became even more important under Islamic rule after it was conquered in A.D. 651. Under the first great Muslim dynasty to rule the region, the Umayyid Caliphate, Merv was a base for conquests further east and later the base of Abassid resistance. After the Abassids defeated the Umayyids and moved their capital to Baghdad, Merv continued to be a centre of Islamic scholarship and the capital of the eastern Islamic Empire. Merv reached its height under the Seljuk Turks; its population in the mid-twelfth century has been estimated at 200,000, among the largest cities in the world at that time: an impressive testimony to its thriving marketplaces, its importance as a strategic military and administrative post, and its essential role as a source of live-sustaining water on the long trek across the desert.

The eclipse of Merv's narrative came at the hands of the Mongol army led by Tolui, son of Genghis Khan. In 1221, something went terribly wrong with what appeared to be peaceful surrender by the city's inhabitants. According to an account written a generation later, the Mongols spared only four hundred valuable artisans and brutally slaughtered the rest of the inhabitants, demolishing the city and its water sources. In the late fourteenth century Tamerlane built the fourth and final city on the site, but it never recovered its past glories.

Bukhara (Uzbekistan)

As the oasis of Merv thins away beneath the dunes, eastbound travellers had a choice of two routes across the desert: to the south-east toward Bactra or to the north-east towards the Sogdian city of Bukhara—located across the Amu Darya in an oasis created by the Zarafshan River. Bukhara had a long tradition of trade as the centre of the cult of Anahita,

The Chor Minar in Bukhara, Uzbekistan, was once the gatehouse to a madrasah. Although the Persian translation is "four minarets" they do not serve this purpose, but interestingly bear Christian, Buddhist and Zoroastrian motifs as well as Islamic ones.

the Iranian goddess of water and fertility. Once each lunar cycle, people of the region came to Bukhara to exchange their idols of the goddess for new ones, a practice so engrained in their culture that it continued even after their conversion to Islam.

Bukhara quickly became a thriving Silk Road marketplace, but it experienced a temporary decline under the nomadic Huns who occupied Sogdiana in the mid-fourth century A.D. Both the Huns and the Sogdians were tolerant of religious diversity, and Bukhara developed a multicultural population as a centre for Jews, Manicheans and Nestorian Christians fleeing the religious persecution of the Persian Sassanid Empire. Today there are still a couple of functioning synagogues in Bukhara, a testament to the lasting role of Jewish merhcants on the Silk Road. Such is the eclectic legacy of the Silk Road on this city that it is said that its population includes more than one hundred and thirty different nationalities.

Like other Sogdian cities, Bukhara was slow to adopt Islam, not converting until the latter part of the eighth century A.D. In 892, it became the capital of the Samanid, a Persian Islamic dynasty that ruled what had once been the eastern Persian Empire from 812-999. Under the Samanids, Bukhara became the intellectual heart of the Islamic world and an important centre of the mystical Sufi sect of Islam. The town grew through cultivation and irrigation so intense that it ran the Zerafshan River dry before it could reach its original destination in the Amu Darya, so that the medieval Persian geographer al-Istakhri described it as being at the "end of the Sogd[ian]'s river."

Although, like most Silk Road cities, the town was surrounded by a protective wall, the army of Genghis Khan destroyed Bukhara in 1220 A.D. Such was the damage caused by the Mongols in the thirteenth century that very few cultural remains survive on the Central Asian part of the Silk Road from the early Islamic period. The Khan himself, however, decided to spare an Islamic architectural masterpiece: the Kalyan Mina-

Far Left Top: Hot Somsa are ready to be served.

Far Left Bottom: Somsa in the traditional tandyr oven. A tandyr is a cylindrical clay or metal oven used in cooking and baking throughout Central Asia as well as in the south Caucasus.

Top Right: A street view of the Kalon Minaret, one of the most prominent landmarks in Bukhara, Uzbekistan".

Left: A silk weaver uses millennia old technology to continue to ply his trade in Bukhara, Uzbekistan.

ret, a stately, graceful tower 47 metres high with a foundation 10 metres deep cushioned on reeds for protection against earthquakes—decorated with 14 ornamental bands of blue tiles that would become the signature colour of Central Asia. And yet until the twentieth century the tower also doubled up as an execution turret, where criminals were cast off to their death, a fact hardly imaginable as one admires its beauty and serenity today.

Samarkand (Uzbekistan)

Beyond Bukhara the traveller reached legendary Samarkand, farther up the Zarafshan River in an even lusher oasis. Established in the seventh century B.C. as Afrasiab, Samarkand was, from its earliest years, a city of craftsmen surrounded by fertile, well-irrigated land. It became the most variegated crossroads of the Silk Road, where as many as six different trading routes came together; a natural place for merchants from either direction to sell their goods.

Samarkand was the principal city of the Sogdian people, who became the greatest traders of the Road, dominating the route from Merv to China, while also establishing a trading network in India and trading directly with Europe. Their Eastern Iranian language was the *lingua franca* of Silk Road merchants from about the second century A.D. until replaced by Persian during the Islamic period. Along with trade goods, the Sogdians exported their religions. Although originally Zoroastrians, at various times they preached Buddhism, Manicheanism, and Christianity, transmitting these religions to China.

A potter moulds his traditional craft in a decorated workshop in Gijduvan, Uzbekistan.

A pomegranate hangs ready to pick. The fruit is symbolic in Central Asia, famous for fertility, abundance and prosperity.

Like Bukhara, Samarkand was a cosmopolitan city that gradually accepted Islam and became a centre of Islamic culture and exquisite architecture, further adorning what was already considered among the most beautiful cities in the world. Unfortunately, little survived the Mongol invasion of 1220. However, unlike most Silk Road cities destroyed by the Mongols, Samarkand experienced a striking resurrection when the next great conqueror, Tamerlane, made it his capital 150 years later.

A brilliant yet ruthless military leader, Tamerlane also had a great appreciation for beauty and culture. That such cruelty and artistic refinement could be embodied in one man is difficult to believe. His invasions turned into bloody looting and kidnapping expeditions in which he brought back captured artisans, scholars, and precious goods to enrich his capital. A European ambassador, Ruy Gonzalez de Clavijo, who arrived in Samarkand in 1404 described a major urban renewal project that tore down houses to build a magnificent central avenue and a remarkable array of "master-craftsmen of all nations" including a thriving silk industry. "The richness and abundance of this great capital" he wrote, "...is indeed a wonder to behold."

Tamerlane's failure to bestow on his successors a long-lasting dynasty has puzzled historians. Though his great-great-great-grandson, Babur, founded the Mughal dynasty in India, which survived until the nineteenth century, the Timurid Empire ceased to exist within a century of his death. It is a consequence of his highly autocratic system of rule that little of permanence was left behind. The loyalty of his subjects was to him rather than his system of government. His power was exercised through him personally rather than through his institutions. He led from the saddle, campaigning to bring glory back home, but did little to formalise the system of rule of the territories he had won.

Miniature glazed clay statues depicting traditional Uzbek clothing stand ready for sale at Chorsu Bazaar in Samarkand.

Today the magnificent Registan—a complex of three Islamic theological schools (madrasas)—dominates the centre of Samarkand as testament to the glory of Tamerlane's triumphs. The first of these schools was founded in 1417 by Ulugh Beg, Tamerlane's grandson and a brilliant astronomer and mathematician. Well before the first madrasa was established, the central square of the Registan was already the great trading centre of the city, where merchants set up their tents in front of a bazaar built by Touman Aka, Tamerlane's youngest wife. The late eighteenth century Chorsu Bazaar behind the Registan continues this tradition today.

Tashkent (Uzbekistan), Khujand (Tajikistan), and the Fergana Valley

A traveller heading north-east out of Samarkand would pass through Tashkent, the modern capital of Uzbekistan, in an oasis formed by the Chirchnik River. The original town, called Chach, was established almost 2,500 years ago and developed into a trading centre between the Sogdians and Turkic nomads. It was an important way station on the northern route of the Silk Road—which continued towards China along the northern edge of the Tien Shan Mountains.

In 1214, the city was sacked by the Khwarezmians, a Persian/Turkish dynasty that had established independence from the Seljuks. Five years later, Genghis Khan finished the destruction. Tashkent began to revive under Tamerlane, and today it is the largest city of Central Asia, with a population over two million, and a major centre of Islamic culture.

The middle route out of Samarkand led to Khujand, about 100 km due south of Tashkent and today separated by the artificial Stalinist border between Uzbekistan and Tajikisitan. Beyond Khujand, the route took the traveller through the broad, fertile Fergana Valley, over the Alai Mountains, and on to Kashgar, just across the western border of modern China. In 329 B.C., Alexander the Great founded his furthest eastern outpost, Alexandria Eschate (Alexandria the Farthest), near the site of Khujand.

As with many cities, Khujand's importance, both historically and today, comes from its location: on the Syr Daria (Jaxartes) River at the head of the Fergana Valley, which played a fundamental role in the history of the Silk Road. There is some evidence that, as early as 250 B.C., the Greco-Bactrian kingdom that followed Alexander's empire sent representatives from Alexandria Eschate through the valley to try and contact the Chinese, perhaps reaching Kashgar or even beyond.

We know for certain that the Chinese representative Zhang Qian arrived in the valley around 128 B.C. on his way to find the Yuezhi, who were then living to the south on the Amu Darya River. Zhang Qian described the valley —which he called the Kingdom of Dayuan—as heavily populated with 300,000 people living in 70 walled cities and rich fields that grew a number of crops unknown to the Chinese: grapes, carrots, garlic, sesame, and a nutritious plant of the pea family called alfalfa, which was used for feeding livestock. More important than the alfalfa were the unusually strong horses that ate it: a breed that became known in China as the "Heavenly Horses" and inspired the Chinese to establish trading relations with the West.

Penjikent, Dushanbe, and the Pamir Highway (Tajikistan)

The third major route out of Samarkand led south to Bactra, which remained a busy crossroads and trading city long after the fall of the Kushan Empire in the third century A.D. Located at the northern end of the Indian Grand Trunk Road, Bactra was the gateway to India. It was also located on a long-established Silk Road route through Afghanistan's Wakhan Corridor as well as a well-travelled alternate route to the northeast that followed the course of the modern Pamir Highway, one of the most dramatic drives in the world.

Top Left: A double humped Bactrian Camel in the Kyzylkum Desert in Uzbekistan.

Bottom Left: Tashkent Inpedendance square, Uzbekistan.

Right: Musician at Juma mosque in Khiva, Uzbekistan.

The highway begins in Mazar-i-Sharif, Afghanistan, near the ruins of Bactra, and runs north though Uzbekistan before turning east through the Tajik capital of Dushanbe. About halfway across the country it makes a deep curve to the south along the Panj River, the primary tributary of the Amu Darya, before heading northward into the mountains. The highway crosses the Pamirs through the Ak-Baital Pass at an elevation of 4,655 metres and continues into Kygyzstan. With more than half of modern Tajikistan above 3,000 metres in elevation it is one of the world's most mountainous countries and yet not even this formidable barrier could prevent trade from permeating.

Silk Road merchants could follow this route or, to avoid the out-of-the way southern curve, take a more direct but difficult shortcut up the precipitous valley of the Vakhsh River, the other major tributary of the Amu Darya. Both routes led to the Irkeshtam Pass on the modern border of Kyrgyzstan and China. Whatever route they took, and wherever they crossed the mountains, traversing the Pamirs—also referred to as the "Roof of the World"—was one of the greatest challenges of the journey.

An alternate route out of Samarkand followed the Zarafshan River valley towards the southeast to Penjikent, now in far western Tajikstan. From there it crossed the rugged Fann Mountains to a junction where the traveller could head north to Khujand and Tashkent or south toward the modern site of Dushanbe, on the route from Bactra to the Irkeshtam Pass.

Penjikent was a relative latecomer to the Silk Road, rising to prominence only in the fifth century A.D. as a wealthy bastion of high Sogdian culture. After being conquered by the Arabs in 722., the city struggled under foreign rule until it was abandoned toward the end of the eighth century A.D. Excavations during the twentieth century discovered a city frozen in time, where extraordinary manuscripts, pottery, sculpture, and wall

paintings (frescoes) were so well preserved that it became known as the Central Asian Pompeii. Today the best of these treasures are found in museums, but the dusty ruins of Penjikent outside the modern city of the same name testify to the rise and fall of a cultured Silk Road city.

The Caspian and Black Sea Route (Turkmenistan and Uzbekistan)

Although most travellers from the west reached Bukhara and Samarkand on the main route through Merv, some took a northern route from ports on the Black and Caspian seas. From the Black Sea, which was accessible by water from Constantinople, this route either crossed the Caspian by boat or curved north of it though the steppes of the present-day Russian Federation and Kazakhstan, before heading south into the Karakum Desert.

There, another oasis city, Konye-Urgench (Old Urgench), developed on the western bank of the ever-benevolent Amu Darya. As with many Central Asian trading centres, the city became one of the major cities of the medieval Islamic world before being destroyed by the army of Genghis Khan. Although the city began to recover, it was abandoned in the late fourteenth century A.D. after the Amu Darya changed its course and Tamerlane, the art-crazed warrior king, finished the destruction, fearing that the once majestic city might eclipse his own beloved capital of Samarkand.

Left: The exquisitely decorated ceiling above the tomb of Tamerlane in Samarkand, Uzbekistan.

Top & Bottom Right: Uzbek flatbread, called lepioshka, is made by hand into a circular shape, before using pins to decorate the surface, and being baked in a traditional tandyr oven.

Beyond Urgench, the route continued south along the Amu Darya, crossed the river, and reached Khiva in modern Uzbekistan. According to legend, Khiva was founded by Noah's son, Shem, who discovered a well with pure water there. The archaeological evidence, however, suggests it was established in the sixth century A.D. and reached prominence during the mid-Islamic period. Although slaves—almost always foreign captives—were bought and sold all along the Silk Road, Khiva became known especially for its slave market, and continued to be a slave centre for Russian slaves until well into the twentieth century. Unlike most Central Asian cities, Khiva was not completely destroyed by Genghis Khan and Tamerlane. Today it is among the best-preserved Silk Road cities, with much of its historic core intact.

At sunset, long after the tour groups have deserted for the day, Khiva's sandstone ramparts encase canyon-like streets between walled courtyards with beautifully sculpted wooden doors. Although a Soviet sanitsation project, the city is quaintly charming and allows perhaps the closest re-telling of the splendour of the Silk Road days. Wherever you try and walk in this citadel, you inevitably end up at the shimmering turquoise Kalta Minor, decorated with glazed tiles and majolica. It may be a nineteenth century relic surrounded by seventeenth century A.D. walls but this does nothing to dampen the wonder or spirit of one of *the* Silk Road cities of Transoxiana.

The faithful gather for evening prayers at the Po-i-Kalyan mosque in Bukhara, Uzbekistan.

A man climbs one of the minarets of the Registan in Samarkand, Uzbekistan. Although the word "registan" typically describes the main squares of many Central Asian cities, the one in Samarkand is becoming as recognisable as Russia's Red Square.

The inside of a nomadic yurt in Kyrgyzstan, filled with all of life's earthly possessions required to live a nomadic existence, beautifully decorated.

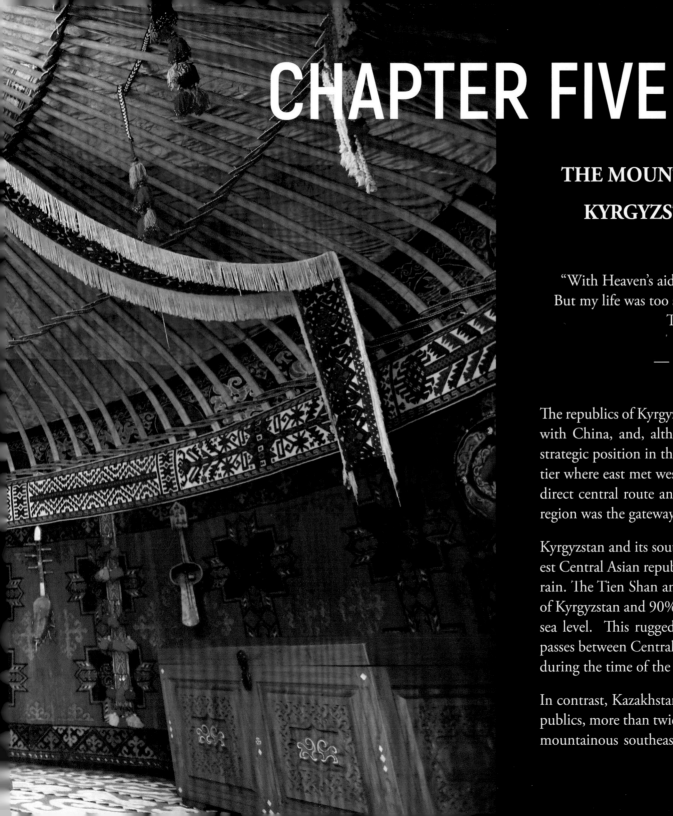

CHAPTER FIVE

THE MOUNTAINS AND THE STEPPES:

KYRGYZSTAN AND KAZAKHSTAN

"With Heaven's aid I have conquered a huge empire for you.
But my life was too short to achieve the conquest of the world.
That task is left for you."

— Genghis Khan to his sons

The republics of Kyrgyzstan and Kazakhstan both share long borders with China, and, although lesser known, they occupied a similar strategic position in the history of the Silk Road—as a distant frontier where east met west. For eastbound Silk Road travellers on the direct central route and the longer, but easier, northern route, this region was the gateway to China.

Kyrgyzstan and its southern neighbour Tajikistan are the two smallest Central Asian republics, and they share similar mountainous terrain. The Tien Shan and Pamir mountain ranges cover almost 65% of Kyrgyzstan and 90% of the land is more than 1,500 metres above sea level. This rugged landscape offers two of the best mountain passes between Central Asia and China, still used today as they were during the time of the Silk Road.

In contrast, Kazakhstan is by far the largest of the Central Asian republics, more than twice as big as the other four combined. From its mountainous southeastern border with Kyrgyzstan and China the terrain transitions to deserts in the central and south-western part of the country and then to the world's largest dry steppe in the north—stretching from the Caspian Sea on the west to the Altai mountains in the east.

The history of these two countries is different from that of Silk Road countries farther south and west. Although some regions were claimed by the ancient Persian Empire, there was little Persian influence on this distant frontier until much later in its history. Alexander stopped short of these lands in his march of conquest, and the great wave of Islam came more slowly. The dominant force in the history of these regions has been the nomads from the north who swept southward across the steppes to raid, conquer, or settle.

Early History

A nomadic, warlike people called the Scythians gained control of the eastern Central Asian steppes and mountain valleys around 750 B.C. They roamed across the Kazakh steppe, with the centre of their culture in a region of south-eastern Kazakhstan and northern Kyrgyzstan called Zhetysyu, literally "seven rivers" for the rivers that flow into Lake Balkhash. Maintaining their nomadic horse culture, the Scythians left no cities; however, they were expert goldsmiths as testified by beautiful jewellery and a full suit of golden armour found in a burial mound (Issyk kurgan) near the former Kazakh capital of Almaty.

Around the second century B.C., a nomadic tribe from the east called the Wusun drove the Scythians out of the Zhetysyu region, including their central location around scenic Lake Issyk Kul in northern Kyrgyzstan. One of the largest alpine lakes in the world, its name means "hot lake" a reference to the fact that it doesn't freeze in winter—probably due to its saline content and its retention of heat from the summer months. The region from Issyk Kul westward along both sides of the modern Kyrgyz–Kazakh border—like the Zhetysu, a well-watered land featuring several

Top & Bottom: A Kyrgyz nomad rounds up his flock at the end of a hard day, near At Bashy, Kyrgyzstan.

river valleys—would become one of the main population centres of the Silk Road.

Two centuries later, in the first century A.D., the Wusun were displaced by the Huns, who dominated the area until they were driven out by Turkic warriors from the northern steppes in 565 A.D. These people, called the Gokturks, established a two-part empire with an Eastern Khanate in Mongolia and a Western Khanate that stretched from Lake Balkhash across the steppes and beyond the Caspian Sea.

The Western Khanate's capital of Suyab (modern-day Ak-Beshim, about 60 km east of the Kyrgyzstan capital, Bishkek) was a major Silk Road city. Such was the confluence of trading cultures, that archaeological excavations have revealed Chinese fortifications, Buddhist temples and statues, a Nestorian Christian church and cemetery, Zoroastrian ossuaries, and Turkic *bal-bals* (anthropomorphic stone funerary monuments). There is also what appears to be a tenth century A.D. Nestorian monastery with frescoes and inscriptions in two Turkic languages: Sogdian and Uyghur.

In 648, Suyab became a military outpost of the Chinese Tang Dynasty, which had expanded its territory west of the Tien Shan Mountains. By the time the Western Khanate collapsed in 744, the Chinese controlled the Issyk Kul region and the Talas River basin of western Kyrgyzstan and southern Kazakhstan. Six years later, the Islamic Abbasid Caliphate defeated the rival Umayyad Caliphate in Iraq and immediately sent an army into Central Asia, setting up an inevitable conflict.

The Battle of Talas

In July of 751, the Chinese and Arab armies met on the Talas River near where it crosses the modern border of Kyrgyzstan and Kazakhstan. This was the only direct military contact between these two great Silk Road powers, but would define whether the history of Central Asia was pre-

Top & Bottom: Scenes of tranquillity from near the Talas River, Kyrgyzstan.

dominantly to be influenced by the Islamic or Chinese world. A Chinese source estimated the Arab force as large as 200,000 soldiers—probably an exaggeration. The estimate of the Chinese force was more accurate: 10,000 Tang soldiers, 20,000 Turkic Karluk mercenaries from what is now eastern Kazakhstan, and an unknown number of Sogdians, who had resisted the Islamic onslaught.

The battle turned when the Karluks and Sogdians changed sides, perhaps seeing the inevitable outcome. In disarray the Chinese fled east of the Tien Shan with what was left of their army; of the 10,000 Tang soldiers, only 2,000 returned to China. The Chinese defeat brought repercussions that reverberated throughout China ultimately leading to an upheaval and revolt against the ruling Tang Dynasty. For a time, the Chinese maintained their influence in the region, but by the end of the eighth century A.D. they were gone and did not cross the Tien Shan again for almost a thousand years.

Perhaps more important than the strategic results of the battle, was the cultural significance. Many Chinese prisoners of war were taken to Samarkand, including artisans who were experts at papermaking, silk weaving, painting, and metalworking. Some paper had already been produced outside of China, but the large-scale technology to manufacture it was unknown. The Chinese papermakers stayed in Samarkand where they shared the technology and helped to establish the first paper mill in the Islamic world, or so the romantic story goes. In 794-95, another paper mill was founded in the Abbasid capital of Baghdad. Whatever the reality, the widespread availability of paper allowed knowledge to be recorded and disseminated more rapidly resulting in an explosion of literature covering science, mathematics and travel.

A lone nomad on horseback is overshadowed by the formidable Tian Shan mountain range in the south of Kyrgyzstan that contains some of the country's highest peaks.

Other Chinese artisans, including the silk weavers, were sent further west, first to Kufa and then to Baghdad (both in modern Iraq). By this time, silk weaving was common from Central Asia to Constantinople, but weavers used imported silk yarn from China. By the middle of the sixth century A.D., the Byzantines had obtained silkworm eggs from travellers on the Silk Road, but the secrets of sericulture (silk production) were guarded so closely that the Byzantine efforts had little effect, and they apparently never discovered how to produce the long filaments required for fine fabric. By now the techniques revealed by the Chinese prisoners led to large-scale production of fine silk yarn. Mulberry trees, which produced the leaves that formed the only diet of the silkworm, quickly became a commercial crop from Central Asia across North Africa and into Spain.

The Rise of Islam

Abbasid influence did not last long in this distant region, and they were soon replaced by the Persian Islamic dynasty of the Samanids, who made Bukhara their capital and transformed it into a great centre of Islamic culture. Despite their connections via the Silk Road, the cities in Kyrgyzstan and Kazakhstan were slower to accept the new religion. The turning point came in 999 when a confederacy of Turkic tribes called the Karakhanids drove the Samanids out of Bukhara.

The Karakhanids were devout Muslims, but unlike the Abbasids and Samanids who conquered from a distance, they came from the steppes of Kazakhstan and centred their empire in the east. At various times, the Karakhanids had capitals at Uzgen in the Fergana Valley, at Balasagun in the Chuy River Valley east of Bishkek, and at Kashgar, the great Silk Road crossroads of western China. Balasagun surpassed Suyab as the major city in the well-populated Chuy Valley and developed into a centre of the newly embraced Islamic religion. Today, its ruins include a field of

A Kazakh eagle hunter. This 4,000 year old tradition is still practised today to hunt foxes and hares. Even though modern rifles could be used to hunt, this is now seen as the highest form of traditional art and dedication.

stone grave markers *(bal-bals)* and the Burana Tower, a minaret that was originally 46 metres tall but has been reduced to 26 metres by a series of earthquakes.

In 1134, Buddhist Mongol invaders called the Khitans conquered the eastern part of the Karakhanid Empire and established their own capital at Balasagun. The relationship between the Buddhist conquerors and their Islamic people was always rocky, and it reached a crisis during the early thirteenth century, when a new ruler banned public Islamic services. By this time Genghis Khan had conquered vast lands to the east, and the people of Balasagun appealed to him for help. In 1218, one of Khan's armies took the capital without a fight and declared religious freedom. They were welcomed as liberators.

The Mongol Invasion

A few decades earlier a large and powerful Turkic-Persian empire, the Khwarezmian dynasty, had developed in the region, establishing its border just east of the Syr Darya, where there were a number of important Silk Road cities. By 1218, Genghis Khan, who now controlled the Silk Road from the Khwarezm frontier deep into China, was eager to trade peacefully with his new neighbour, who also ruled richer cities including Bukhara, Samarkand, Balkh, and Merv. In response to this interest, traders from Bukhara journeyed to the Khan's court in Mongolia, carrying beautiful textiles and other goods. The Khan rewarded the merchants handsomely and sent 450 Muslim traders and camel drivers in a great caravan. According to one of Genghis Khan's historical biographers, Ralph Fox, "Its five hundred camels carried nuggets of gold and silver, silk, ... the furs of beaver and sable, and many ingenious and elegant articles of Chinese workmanship."

When the caravan reached the Khwarezm frontier city of Otrar in south-eastern Kazakhstan, the governor ordered all of the travellers killed

The striking Bayterek Tower, on the Nurzhol Boulevard in Kazakhstan's capital of Nur-Sultan is seen as a symbol of the country's independence.

as spies and confiscated their goods. Still hoping to trade, the Khan sent three ambassadors, two Mongols and one Muslim, directly to the Shah in his capital at Samarkand, demanding that the governor be given to him for punishment. Instead the Shah ordered the men's hair and beards shaved—a ritual insult—and sent the head of the Muslim ambassador back to Khan with the Mongols.

Located on a large oasis at the junction of routes leading to China, Persia, and the Eurasian steppes, Otrar was among the great Silk Road cities, but now it was a palpable target for revenge. In 1219 A.D., Genghis Khan led an army of between 100,000 and 200,000 warriors through Kazakhstan toward the heart of the Silk Road. The Khwarezm army was even larger, but the Shah was afraid to meet the Mongols in open battle and instead spread his army among his many cities.

While Genghis Khan orchestrated the destruction of Bukhara, an army led by two of his sons laid siege to Otrar, a new military technique that the Mongols had learned from the Chinese. After six months, they destroyed the city and slaughtered all its inhabitants. The governor's punishment was suitably orchestrated, being killed by having molten silver poured into his eyes and ears. Although Genghis Khan had originally intended only to trade with the West, this marked the beginning of the westward invasions that would wreak destruction all along the Silk Road. As the twelfth century Persian historian Ata-Malik Juvaini wrote, the injudicious action of the governor of Otrar had not only destroyed a caravan but "laid waste a whole world."

Unlike many cities destroyed by the Mongols, Otrar recovered and was once again a thriving trading centre by the mid-thirteenth century. In the late fourteenth century, it became part of the empire of Tamerlane, who died there in 1405 while gathering troops for an invasion of China. Today, Otrar is reduced to a dusty archaeological site, but its ruins reveal

a well-organised, densely populated trading city in the transitional zone between nomads of the northern steppe and sedentary populations of the south.

The Central and Northern Routes

The broad, fertile Fergana Valley, which played such an integral role in the history of the Silk Road, lies today in parts of Uzbekistan, Tajikistan, and Kyrgyzstan, although during the days of the Silk Road it was more unified. The central route of the Silk Road ran through the valley, from Khujand (in modern Tajikistan) to the ancient city of Osh (in modern Kyrgyzstan). Believed to be 2,500-3,000 years old, the city of Osh was a crossroads where the central trading route met a north-south route from Talas (modern Taraz, Kazakhstan). From Osh, the route continued south toward the village of Sary Tash high in the Pamir Mountains at an elevation of 3,170 metres. Today, this route forms part of the Pamir Highway and most traffic continues towards Tajikistan. During the days of the Silk Road, however, travellers largely headed east from Sary Tash to cross the Irkeshtam Pass into China.

Left: A horse grazes near the Tien Shan mountains in the south-east of Kazakhstan.

Top & Bottom Right: A traditional caravanserai sits nestled in the mountains aside a river providing the perfect resting space for Silk Road merchants.

The northern route led from the city of Tashkent to Shymkent in southern Kazakhstan. There the road forked, with one branch leading to the northwest up the Syr Darya River toward the steppes and the other heading eastwards to China. Shymkent was founded in the twelfth century as a caravanserai to protect the nearby city of Sayram, a trading centre believed to be 3,000 years old. Although a caravanserai was primarily a place for merchants to rest and trade, it could also serve as a fortification. In time Shymkent developed into a thriving market in its own right, where nomadic tribes came to trade with the settled farming and urban people. Although destroyed several times in the past, beginning with the invasion of Genghis Kahn, Shymkent today is one of the largest cities in modern Kazakhstan with a population of around one million.

From Shymkent, the route to China led to Talas on the Talas River, near the site of the Battle of Talas. Dating back to a fort built in the first century B.C., Talas emerged as a major fortified city on the Silk Road in the sixth century A.D. With abundant water from the river and fertile soil it became the centre of a city-state that fell under the domain of various powers, similar to many Silk Road cities. Like Shymkent it survived the Mongol invasion to become a large modern metropolis, called Taraz today.

Beyond Talas, the road crossed the present-day border and passed through Suyab and Balasagun to Lake Issyk-Kul, where the traveller faced a key choice. He could continue travelling eastward around the lake and follow the northern curve of the Tien Shan Mountains—a route the Chinese called the Tien Shan Pei Liu (Road North of the Celestial Mountains). This was the easiest of all Silk Road routes, for it had water and relatively flat elevations that could be travelled by wagons. However, it was seldom used as the main route, due to threats from the nomadic tribes of the steppes, who would steal the merchants' goods and livestock and kill or capture the travellers.

▶ *Big Almaty Lake, with its characteristic turquoise hue, is located 28 kilometres south of Almaty, Kazakhstan.*

The safer, if more difficult, route headed south into the mountains, through the modern city of Naryn on the Naryn River, the source of the Syr Daria. Some 125 km south of Naryn is the Tash Rabat Caravanserai, one of the best preserved medieval stone structures on the Silk Road, featuring a large domed building with about 30 smaller rooms around it, all set within a square walled compound. Although most scholars believe the structure was built in the fifteenth century specifically as a haven for travellers, some think that it may date back to a tenth century Nestorian monastery.

Beyond Tash Rabat, the traveller crossed the Torugart Pass, still an important entry point into China today. Whether Silk Road merchants used this pass or the Irkeshtam Pass to the south, the road led to Kashgar, the gateway to China.

The Syr Darya and the Aral Sea

The north-western road from Shymkent along the Syr Darya featured a series of important cities including Otrar, the city that set off the Mongol invasion, and Turkistan, which replaced Otrar as the major commercial centre in the area. Turkistan was home to a twellfth century Sufi mystic named Khoja Ahmad Yasavi who made it an important place of Islamic learning for the people of the steppe. In the late fourteenth century, Tamerlane had a beautiful blue-domed mausoleum built over Yasavi's grave, and the city remains a place of pilgrimage today.

Beyond Otrar and Turkestan was the fortress city of Sauran, which was occupied until the eighteenth century and today is among the best preserved archaeological sites in Kazakhstan. Archaeologists have found evidence that the people of Sauran and Turkistan used an underground irrigation system called a *karez*, which combined a series of wells with underground channels. Originally developed in pre-Islamic Persia, where they were called *qanats*, the technology was passed from west to east

A seamstress adds the finishing touches to a felt rug symbolic of Kyrgyzstan's nomadic culture.

along the Silk Road. *Karez* are also found as far away as Mongolia and North Africa.

Although Sauran and Turkistan are both located near the Syr Darya, the need for underground water supplies illustrates the precarious nature of even the largest rivers in the deserts and dry steppes of Central Asia. Rising as the Naryn River in the Tien Shan Mountains of Kyrgyzstan, the Syr Darya generally carries plenty of water through the Fergana Valley, where another major tributary called the Kara Darya meets the Naryn River to form the main channel. However, as it turns towards the north through drier lands the flow dissipates until the river almost disappears, short of its traditional destination in the Aral Sea, once the fourth largest lake in the world. The same fate is true of the Amu Darya river to the south, which thanks to Uzbek over irrigantion literally disappears into the land.

Even in Silk Road times, the downstream flow of these rivers was greatly impacted by irrigation and other human needs, but major Soviet irrigation projects begun in the early 1960s have turned the Aral Sea into an ecological disaster. By 2007, the sea had shrunk to 10% of its normal size, divided into northern and southern parts. The northern part has begun to recover due to a large dam built by the Kazakhstan government from its significant oil revenue. Across the border to the south, in Uzbekistan, little progress has been made, however. The demand Uzbeks have on the resources of the Amu Darya continues unabated – without the water upstream farmers would be unemployed. In 2015 the eastern basin of the south Aral Sea completely dried up. The government have turned to finding oil and gas on the seabed, assuming it to be a lost cause. It is arguably one of the greatest environmental disasters of our time.

A modern-day nomad rides in the Kazakh mountains.

Nomadic Culture

The interaction between nomadic tribes and sedentary farmers and city dwellers was an ongoing feature of Silk Road history. The devastating Mongol attacks on the great trading cities were the most violent and dramatic of these interactions, but there were many peaceful contacts too. Nomads roamed the broad steppe in what is the northern part of modern Kazakhstan and came to trade with cities in the south. The city people provided them with grain and handcrafted goods in return for horses and other livestock—and as long as this trading partnership was maintained, the relationship usually remained peaceful.

Archaeological evidence suggests that the symbiotic relationship between nomads and sedentary people dates back to the Iron Age. Rich Scythian gravesites have been found near ancient agricultural settlements, and archaeologists believe that the Scythians made a "deal" with the farmers and city dwellers: promising not to attack them in return for watching over the graves of their elite.

This nomadic heritage is still reflected in both Kazakhstan and Kyrgyzstan, where traditional *yurts*—moveable, felt-covered homes—can be seen on the steppes and in mountain valleys. The nomads were people of the horse, and this heritage remains in the national cuisines, with horsemeat and mare's milk added to the traditional mutton and sheep's milk of other Central Asian countries.

Traditional sports of the steppe are still practiced as well. Hunting with golden eagles dates back thousands of years, as testified by Bronze Age petroglyphs and the discovery of a golden eagle in an ancient tomb in western Kazakhstan. The closely guarded secrets of the *berkutchi* (eagle hunter) are passed from father to son. Today, the Syugaty Valley, 150 km east of Almaty, is the centre of Kazakh eagle hunting.

Nomadic culture is also best seen today in its many sports and games that have survived time. Buzkhashi, literally "grabbing the dead goat," is a wild, rough game played on horseback, focused on a *boz* made of the carcass of a calf, goat or sheep. Although there are many formats, the basic purpose is to pick up the animal, ride away from one's opponents, and carry the *boz* to the goal. Today the game is played throughout Central Asia in settings ranging from stadiums to the open steppes and in verdant valleys where the might of the towering mountains looks on. Although it originated in the north, Buzkhashi is also the national sport of Afghanistan—another cultural tradition that was transferred along the Silk Road.

Left: Rock carvings, or petroglyphs, from Saimaluu Tash in Kyrgyzstan. Over 10,000 carved pictures have been identified. They are sacred displays of offerings of the ancient people from the valley.

Right: A nomadic Kyrgyz horse rider grabs the carcass of a goat from the ground during a local game of Buzkashi in Issyk Kul, Kyrgyzstan.

▶ *A renovated part of the Great Wall of China, near Beijing. The "Wall"*
is a collection of fortification systems built across the historically northern
Chinese borders to protect against various nomadic groups of the steppe.

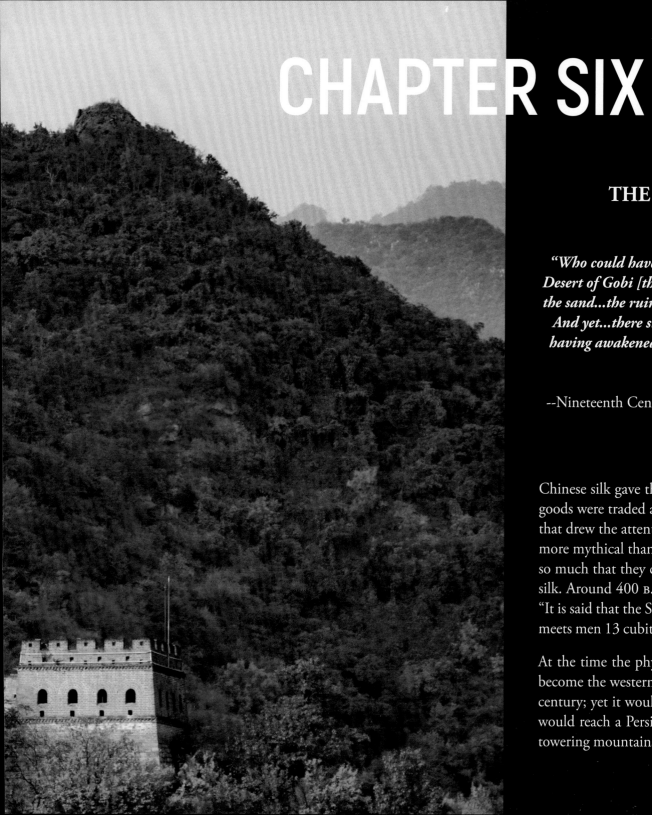

CHAPTER SIX

THE LAND OF SILK: CHINA

"Who could have imagined that in the interior of the dreaded Desert of Gobi [the Taklamakan], actual cities slumbered under the sand...the ruined survivals of a once flourishing civilisation? And yet...there stood I like the prince in the enchanted wood, having awakened to new life the city which had slumbered for a thousand years."

--Nineteenth Century Explorer Sven Hedin upon discovering the ancient city of Loulan.

Chinese silk gave the Silk Road its name, and although many other goods were traded along the Road, it was this precious, exotic fabric that drew the attention of the West to a distant land that was at first more mythical than real. This product enthralled the ancient Greeks so much that they called the Chinese *Seres* from the Greek word for silk. Around 400 B.C., a Greek physician at the Persian court wrote, "It is said that the Seres and the Northern Indians are so tall that one meets men 13 cubits [6 metres] high; they live more than 200 years."

At the time the physician wrote, trade along the routes that would become the western Silk Road had been flourishing for more than a century; yet it would be three centuries before a Chinese delegation would reach a Persian court. Nomadic warriors, brutal deserts, and towering mountains separated the Chinese heartland from the West.

The Chinese would have to conquer all these barriers before they could join the great Eurasian trading network that was also developing.

Due to the many inter-connecting routes, some lost over time, it is impossible to accurately measure the length of the Silk Road. However, the direct distance "as the crow flies" between modern Istanbul, Turkey and Xi'an, China—the eastern terminus of the Road—is almost exactly 7,000 km. Of that distance, 3,000 km are within the boundaries of modern China. It is no wonder that many accounts of the Silk Road begin and end within this country. During the heyday of the Silk Road, this vast area was characterized by two separate and distinct regions, a division that can still be seen today.

To the east are fertile plains and plateaus watered by the Yellow River (Huang He) and its tributaries, the cradle of Chinese civilization and the centre of political power and expansion. This was the homeland of the Han people, the area protected by the Great Wall in the north. Although various empires expanded beyond this area, it was always the heart of China throughout the Silk Road period.

In the west of the country is a dry, desolate region called the Tarim Basin, dominated by the fearsome Taklamakan Desert. About 1,500 km long from east to west and 600 km from north to south at its widest part, the basin was occupied by city-states centred on oases that provided relief from the relentless desert. Between these oasis cities, travellers faced one of the most inhospitable regions in the world. Today the basin is part of the Xinjiang Uyghur Autonomous Region, which comprises one sixth of China's total area and maintains an independent cultural identity. As the name suggests, almost half the people are Uyghurs, a Turkic ethnic group related to the Turkic peoples of Central Asia.

Sand dunes of the Taklamakan desert ("The Place of No Return") in Xinjiang, China.

Farmers and Nomads

The people of the Yellow River region began growing millet and rice as early as 7000 B.C. Over the following millennia, a sedentary agricultural society continued to develop, becoming more sophisticated and complex. The secret of sericulture, the production of raw silk from the silkworm, was discovered around 2700 B.C. According to one legend, the, Empress Lei Tzu mistakenly dropped a silkworm cocoon in her tea and when she took it out, the cocoon had unwound into one long silk filament. In time, the Chinese produced beautiful silk garments and textiles that would become renowned throughout the world.

While the agricultural society grew in the southeast of China, people on the northern steppes continued to live a nomadic life, herding cattle, sheep, and horses. This same dichotomy of northern nomadic herdsmen and southern sedentary farmers was found throughout Eurasia and actually played a pivotal role in the history of the Silk Road. Although there was conflict between these groups everywhere, it was particularly acute in China, where the transition from the northern steppes to the fertile plains is relatively flat and easy to traverse, making farming settlements and cities more vulnerable to nomadic raids.

Around 600 B.C., steppe nomads perfected the art of horseback riding; by the mid fourth century B.C., they learned how to shoot arrows while riding, developing the first cavalry. This forced the Chinese to form their own cavalry, which required stronger horses and larger herds than they were able to breed themselves. It also forced them to build fortifications to protect their northern border thereby cementing the foundations of what would later become known as the Great Wall of China. During the "Warring States Period" (c. 475-221 B.C.), the three northern states built further walls, which were joined and expanded during the Qin Dynasty (221-206 B.C.), the first imperial dynasty of a united China.

A typical Chinese Imperial roof decoration on a temple.

Beyond the wall, the Chinese faced two powerful nomadic confederacies that shaped Chinese political and military policy. The Xiongnu were a warlike people who roamed the steppes to the north and regularly raided Chinese villages and towns. Despite lavish gifts of silk and princesses, interspersed with military expeditions, the Xiongnu remained the greatest threat to the Chinese heartland. By 200 B.C., they controlled the northern steppes from far eastern Asia to the Aral Sea.

The Yuezhi confederacy lived in the eastern Tarim Basin and the Hexi or Ganshu Corridor (modern Ganshu Province), a semi-arid region that connects China to the Tarim and would become the major route of the Chinese Silk Road. The Yuezhi maintained a friendly trading relationship with the Chinese, providing them with jade, which the Chinese prized even more highly than gold. They also supplied decent horses that the Chinese desperately needed to fight the Xiongnu.

Zhang Qian's Journey to the West

The short-lived Qin Dynasty was followed by the Han Dynasty (202 B.C. to A.D. 220.), which ruled China for more than four centuries and opened the Silk Road to the West. In 140 B.C., Emperor Wu took the throne and attacked the Xiongnu; although he was able to drive them away from the border, the nomads continued their raids. When Xiongnu prisoners reported conflicts between the Xiongnu and Yuezhi, Wu decided to send an emissary to forge a military alliance with the Yuezhi to attack the Xiongnu.

In 138 B.C., a young military officer named Zhang Qian set off with a caravan of about a hundred men and a Xiongnu prisoner named Ganfu, a skilled archer who knew the steppe well. Although the Chinese apparently did not know it, the Xiongnu had driven the Yuezhi out of the Tarim and Hexi Corridor, and they captured Zhang Qian's caravan early in its journey. The prisoners were forced to live and travel with the Xiongnu

CHAPTER SIX **THE LAND OF SILK** 113

for ten years, during which time Zhang Qian was given a Xiongnu wife who bore him a son.

Finally escaping, Zhang Qian, along with his wife, his servant Ganfu, and some of his men, looked for the Yuezhi in the Ili River Valley north of the Tien Shan mountains—which would later become one of the northern routes of the Silk Road. Discovering that the Yuezhi had moved further west, he headed southwest along the rim of the Tarim Basin and over the Pamir Mountains, reaching the Kingdom of Dayuan in the fertile Fergana Valley (today situated between eastern Uzbekistan, southern Kyrgyzstan and northern Tajikistan).

The king of Dayuan had heard of China as a wealthy land and graciously welcomed the travellers. Zhang Qian saw crops he had never seen before, including grapes that were made into delicious wine. Even more remarkable was a powerful breed of horses that he believed might be related to the "Heavenly Horses" described in Chinese legend. These were bigger and stronger than the Chinese horses, and their hooves wore down much more slowly—a great advantage in warfare. Adding to their mythic appeal, the fearsome Fergana horses appeared to sweat blood, which led the Chinese to call them "blood-sweating horses", though it is now thought that this was probably the result of a parasitic infection.

Left: A Chinese farmer carries a yoke with rice grains. The agricultural way of life, centred around rice, has played an important part in China's history for over 3,000 years.

Top Right: Handwoven silk shawls on display at the Sunday Market in Kashgar, China.

Bottom Right: A Uyghur market seller displays his fresh fruit at the Sunday Market in Kashgar, China.

The King of Dayuan ordered that Zhang Qian be escorted south into Sogdiana, where he received another escort to the new land of the Yuezhi on the northern bank of the Amu Darya River. Although they boasted 100,000 to 200,000 horsemen-archers, the Yuezhi were not interested in fighting the even larger army of the Xiongnu, who had recently defeated them. Adding to the Yuezhi king's recalcitrance was the fact that his father had been beheaded and his skull made into a drinking cup for the king of the Xiongnu.

Frustrated in his mission, Zhang Qian visited the markets of Bactra across the river, where he saw a species of bamboo and a type of cloth, probably silk, that originated in the Shu region (modern Sichuan Province) of south-western China. He was told that these items came from a land to the south called Shendu (India). Clearly, there was another route from China (and other countries in the East) to the West.

After a year among the Yuezhi, Zhang Qian headed home. Hoping to avoid the Xiongnu, he travelled along the southern edge of the Tarim Basin on what would become one of the major routes of the Silk Road. Nonetheless he was captured once again by the Xiongnu, who had expanded well south of their homeland. This time he escaped within a year and along with his wife and his faithful companion Ganfu—all that remained of the hundred men who set out twelve years earlier—arrived back at the emperor's court in 125 B.C.

Zhang Qian not only told the emperor of what he had seen with his own eyes, but also what he had learned of even further lands—India, whose armies fought with war elephants; Parthia (Persia), which made beautiful glassware and created silver coins with the face of their king; and a distant sea that apparently referred to the Mediterranean. Emperor Wu was fascinated by all he heard and became more determined than ever to subdue the Xiongnu and provide safe travel to and from the West.

Taking tea at a traditional Uyghur cafe in Hotan, China.

Opening the Road

Emperor Wu renewed his military offensive against the Xiongnu and drove them out of the Hexi Corridor in 121 B.C. To provide safety for travellers, he established military outposts through the corridor and extended the Great Wall to the Gate of Jade (Yumenguan, west of Dunhuang), a mountain pass that marked the entry to the Tarim Basin. In order to survive in these distant outposts, soldiers were sent with their families and farming equipment, to establish farms on the oases when they weren't fighting the nomads. Later, these military settlements spread even further west beyond the wall, increasing the population of the oasis cities along the edges of the Taklamakan Desert and providing the necessary staging posts to encourage merchants and travellers along the Silk Road.

Of all that Zhang Qian reported, Emperor Wu was most interested in the blood-sweating horses of Dayuan. He sent numerous embassies with little effect; the people of Dayuan were willing to offer other goods in trade but would not part with their precious horses. Finally, in 103 B.C., Wu sent a huge army, described by the contemporary Chinese historian Sima Qian as comprised of "60,000 men not counting those who followed as carriers of extra provisions; 100,000 oxen [for food]; more than 30,000 horses, myriads of donkeys, mules and camels, and a commissariat well stocked with supplies besides cross-bows and other arms." After a 40-day siege, the people of Dayuan provided 30 heavenly horses and 3,000 lesser horses. Although only a third survived the return journey, they were enough to establish an Imperial breeding program.

Not long before the attack on Dayuan, sometime between 115 and 105 B.C., a Chinese ambassador with a caravan of silk and other goods travelled all the way to Parthia (Persia), which had a direct trading relationship with Rome. The Parthians welcomed the Chinese with an

A group of tourists mimic an ancient camel caravan at the Ming Sha sand dunes near Dunhuang, China.

escort of 20,000 men, and sent an envoy with trade goods to China in return. For the first time, the Silk Road was open from East to West.

Keeping the Road Open

From the Chinese perspective, the key to keeping the Silk Road open for trade was control over the Tarim Basin. In order to accomplish this, they not only had to subdue the Xiongnu but also establish control over numerous city-states that had developed around the oases. According to the *History of the Later Han (Hou Hanshu)*, written in the fifth century A.D., there were 36 kingdoms in what the Chinese called the "Western Regions" when the Silk Road was first opened during the time of Emperor Wu. Most of these kingdoms were never fully part of China, but during periods of Chinese control they offered tribute to the Emperor and served as military allies. The Xiongnu, Kushans, Tibetans, Turkic tribes, and Mongols controlled at least some of these city-states at various times. The military power in control not only impacted access and safety for travellers but also the taxes merchants had to pay to each kingdom through which they passed.

Early in the first century A.D., just as distant Rome was developing a voracious appetite for Chinese silk, the Xiongnu regained control of the basin. By A.D. 76, the Chinese emperor was ready to abandon the region, but one capable general, Ban Chao—with a small army and the help of merchants—established full control 12 years later and was made Protector General of the Western Regions. Looking to further expand Chinese trade, he sent an emissary named Gan Ying in search of "Da Qin" (Da meaning "Great" and "Qin" being the name of China's founding dynasty). Da Qin was the name the Chinese gave to the mysterious, silk-consuming empire west of Persia, the famed Roman Empire. Gan Ying reached as far as the "Western Sea," probably the Persian Gulf. There, local people told him that the journey to Da Qin was dangerous and

would take him years, prompting Gan Ying to return home. The Persians carried out a lucrative trade of providing Chinese goods to Rome and they had no intention of sharing their secrets with the Chinese.

The victory of General Ban Chao was temporary, and for the next five centuries, as dynasties rose and fell, China struggled to protect the Silk Road. Nonetheless, the exchange of goods and ideas continued. During the northern Wei Dynasty (A.D. 386-535), the government strictly controlled silk manufacturing, only permitting fine silk cloth to be worn by members of the Chinese court and foreign rulers, including those of the steppe—who considered silk clothing a mark of legitimacy. Government silk fabrics could also be provided to Buddhist monasteries, but only by the ruling elite. These laws made silk fabrics imported from Persia (woven from Chinese thread) very popular. Persian silks were wider than Chinese cloth, had larger designs, and were not controlled by the government. This is the period when Buddhism took hold in China, and the Buddhist belief in giving gifts to monasteries further stimulated Chinese interest in foreign luxury goods, including incense and precious gemstones.

China entered a new, golden age under the Tang Dynasty (A.D. 618-907), which not only gained control of the Tarim Basin but also extended its territory beyond the Pamir Mountains into present-day Kyrgyzstan and Kazakhstan. For the first time since the Silk Road was opened under the Han Dynasty, goods (and merchants) flowed freely through the Tarim Basin, as well as along the easier route north of the Tien Shan Mountains—which was more exposed to nomadic attack than the Tarim

Left: A street food seller prepares a tasty meal for passers-by in Urumqi, China.

Top & Bottom Right: Market sellers at a street-side market in Lanzhou, China.

routes. Caravans of camels arrived regularly outside the gates of the Great Wall and even ordinary people could enjoy imported grape wine in glass goblets accompanied by music played on imported lutes. Like the Wei, the Tang controlled silk making, and only the highest officials could wear purple silk, a tradition borrowed, perhaps, from the Byzantine and Persian Empires.

A Crossroads of World Religions

The early Tang Dynasty was also a time of religious freedom, when many religions that had travelled along the Silk Road flourished in China, alongside the native traditions of Confucianism and Taoism. Although Buddhism was by far the strongest of these imported religions, Zoroastrians, Manichaeans, Nestorian Christians, and Jews all made their mark far from the lands of their origins. Many of their practising believers were foreign, their fates often tied to those of the expatriate merchant communities themselves, but they were valued members of society for more than just their religious attitudes, but also their worldly knowledge of subjects ranging from astrology to medicine.

Manichaeism, founded in Persia during the third century A.D., synthesized aspects of many faiths including Christianity, Judaism, Greek mystery religions, Zoroastrianism, and Buddhism. Manichees arrived in China in the late seventh century and established two temples in the Tang capital of Chang'an. In 762, the Uyghur Khan, a close Tang ally, met a Manichaean priest in the city, and the Khan and all his people converted, establishing Manichaeism as the official religion in the vast Uyghur Khanate, which included Mongolia and parts of the Tarim Basin.

Nestorian Christianity emerged in the West between 428-431 when Nestorius, the Patriarch of Constantinople, declared a complete separation between the divine and human natures of Christ. Condemned as a heresy by the Orthodox Church, Nestorianism was soon established

A precipitous winding road provides vital links to village communities in the mountains of Hunan Province, China.

among the Christian community in Persia and reached China through a Persian believer in 635. Nestorian churches were built in major Chinese cities, and the religion flourished until the reign of Emperor Wuzong (840-46), who launched a persecution of "foreign religions" aimed primarily at Buddhism but also targeting Nestorianism, Manichaeism, and Zoroastrianism.

Although Wuzong was influenced by Confucian ministers and his personal belief in Taoism, the driving force behind this persecution was economic. Buddhist temples housed enormous tax-exempt wealth, while Buddhist monks produced no products except spiritual satisfaction for believers. In 845, Wuzong ordered the destruction of 4,600 Buddhist monasteries and 40,000 hermitages, and forced a quarter of a million Buddhist monks and nuns to give up their monastic lives. Nestorianism, Manichaeism and Zoroastrianism were suppressed because they were the religions of Sogdian merchants who dominated Silk Road trade. Manichaeism was of special concern as the state religion of the Uyghurs who were eager to gain a share of the Silk Road trade and provided a threat to Chinese dominance. Although the final and most draconian persecution only lasted 20 months, until Wuzong's death, these religions, and especially Buddhism, never regained their previous dominance, and went into a steep decline before disappearing by the end of the fourteenth century A.D. The preserved ruins of Nestorian churches can still be found in modern Xi'an, site of the former capital of Chang'an.

During this period, the Jewish community in China was not large enough to cause concern, while Islam escaped the persecution because it had not yet become an economic force. That would change within a century.

Islam came to China just before the Tang Dynasty. Arab traders were already used to the seagoing Spice Route before A.D. 500, with their activities focused on the southern port of Guangzhou (better known in

A golden Buddha watches peacefully over visitors to a Chinese temple.

Lake Namtso, in China, hosts a traditional Buddhist festival on its shores. Its cave hermitages have been a destination for Tibetan pilgrims for centuries.

the West as Canton). The first Islamic ambassadors may have arrived as early as 618-20, while the Prophet Mohammed was still alive. However Chinese Muslim tradition points to a delegation that arrived by sea in 651, travelled to the Tang capital of Chang'an, and invited the Emperor Yung Wei to convert to the newly revealed religion. Although Yung Wei declined the invitation, he gave permission to preach Islam throughout his realm and ordered the construction of China's first mosque in Guangzhou. The "Memorial Mosque" that still stands in the city was probably built in the later Tang Dynasty on the site of this first mosque.

Unlike Central Asia, where Islamic armies swept through the land like a religious tidal wave, the religion spread throughout China more gradually. There was no military invasion but Muslim teachers, traders, and settlers continued to arrive by the Spice Route and the Silk Road. By the Song Dynasty (960-1279), Muslim merchants dominated the trade routes, which both strengthened their place in the Chinese empire and spread their religious beliefs.

Islam reached a new level of influence under the Mongol rulers of the Yuan Dynasty, who were not only tolerant but pragmatic. As foreigners themselves, they saw the Muslims as an opportunity to dilute the strength of the Han population. Hundreds of thousands of Muslims from Central Asia—Persians, Arabs, Uyghurs, and other ethnic groups—moved, either voluntarily or by force, into China to help the Mongols administer and develop their Chinese empire. They became tax collectors, financial officers, and businessmen. Just as they did along the western routes of the Silk Road, Muslim scholars brought new scientific and technical knowledge, including astronomy and architecture.

Buddhist prayer flags flap in the wind near Tibet, China. Tibetans believe that the prayers written on the flags will be blown by the wind to spread goodwill and compassion.

The Mongols and the Black Death

Genghis Khan united the Mongol tribes in 1206 and that same year launched an attack on the Western Xia Dynasty (1038-1227), which controlled northern Chinese lands adjacent to Mongolia. China was divided during this period, and the Western Xia was one of three ruling dynasties. Next the Mongol leader pushed south to attack the Jin Dynasty (1115-1234) in the traditional heart of China. In 1215, aided by siege technology employed by Chinese and Muslim engineers, he captured and sacked the Jin capital of Yamjing (modern Beijing) and forced the emperor to flee toward the south. Now in control of northern China, Genghis Khan turned his attention to the west, where he embarked on his infamous campaign of destruction along the Silk Road.

The battle for China was not over, however, and it was not until 1279, more than half a century after the death of Genghis Khan, that his descendants gained full control over the "Middle Kingdom" by conquering the Chinese Song Dynasty (960-1279) in the south. During this conflict, both sides used gunpowder technology that had been developed by the Song and was taught to the Mongols by northern Chinese soldiers. Eight years before the fall of the Song in 1279, Kublai Khan, a grandson of Genghis Khan, established the Yuan Dynasty with its capital at Beijing. Khan's reign ushered in the "Pax Mongolica" (Mongol Peace), a period when the Mongols controlled the entire length of the Silk Road. It was said that at this time, "a maiden bearing a nugget of gold on her head could wander safely throughout the realm."

Marco Polo made his famous trip to China during this peaceful period. Polo's father and uncle had met Kublai Khan on an earlier trip, and the journey with his son, Marco, was in fulfilment of the Great Khan's request for direct communication with the Pope. The Polos arrived sometime between 1271 and 1275 and stayed until 1292. In *The Travels of Marco Polo*, the wonders of Kublai Khan's palace are described:

> *"You must know that it is the greatest Palace that ever was... The roof is very lofty, and the walls of the Palace are all covered with gold and silver. They are also adorned with representations of dragons [sculptured and gilt], beasts and birds, knights and idols, and sundry other subjects. And on the ceiling too you see nothing but gold and silver and painting. The Hall of the Palace is so large that it could easily dine 6,000 people; and it is quite a marvel to see how many rooms there are besides. The building is altogether so vast, so rich, and so beautiful, that no man on earth could design anything superior to it."*

After less than a century of power, the Mongols were overthrown by the native Chinese Ming Dynasty in 1368. Among the factors that drove the Chinese to revolt was a devastating plague that became known as the Black Death, which originated in China during the early 1330s. Given China's active trading with the West during the *Pax Mongolica*, it's unclear why the plague took more than a decade to reach Europe, but it was probably carried along the Silk Road by Mongol warriors and traders. In 1347 a Mongol army suffering from the plague besieged the Genoese trading city of Caffa on the Black Sea in modern Ukraine and catapulted infected bodies over the city walls. The Genoese merchants fled by ship and brought the plague to Naples, from where it spread like a wildfire throughout Europe.

The plague killed between one third and one half of the European population and was almost as devastating in Egypt and the Middle East. In China it continued to cause a dramatic population loss that had begun with famine caused by the destruction of farming activities by Mongol warriors. From the beginning of the Mongol invasion to the end of the Yuan Dynasty, the Chinese population dropped from about 120 million to 60 million.

The rapid spread of the plague offered clear, if sobering, testimony to the power of the great overland trading networks that had been established between China and the Mediterranean. Yet by the time of the plague, the importance of the Silk Road had already begun to decline as the route by sea became safer due to better and stronger ships. Although the sea route faced its own dangers of storms and pirates, it was much cheaper to trade directly with China, bypassing the inflated prices that middlemen charged to carry goods on each stage of the Silk Road. The death knell of the Silk Road came in 1517, when the first Portuguese ship arrived in Canton.

The Routes through China

There were three primary Silk Road routes through China's Western Region. All of these began at the Chinese capital of Chang'an (modern Xi'an) and headed north-west through the Hexi Corridor to the eastern part of the Tarim Basin. There they split, with one route running south of the Taklamakan Desert, another running to the north of the desert, and the third heading further north, around the Tien Shan Mountains and into the steppe.

Chang'an and the Imperial Road

Chang'an was established as the Chinese capital around 200 B.C. by Emperor Liu Bang, founder of the Han Dynasty. Liu Bang originally made his capital further east at Luoyang, which the Chinese believed to be the centre of the world. He decided to build a new capital on the Wu River, near the western frontier where the Xiongnu posed the greatest threat to Chinese security. The fertile, well-protected Wu basin is

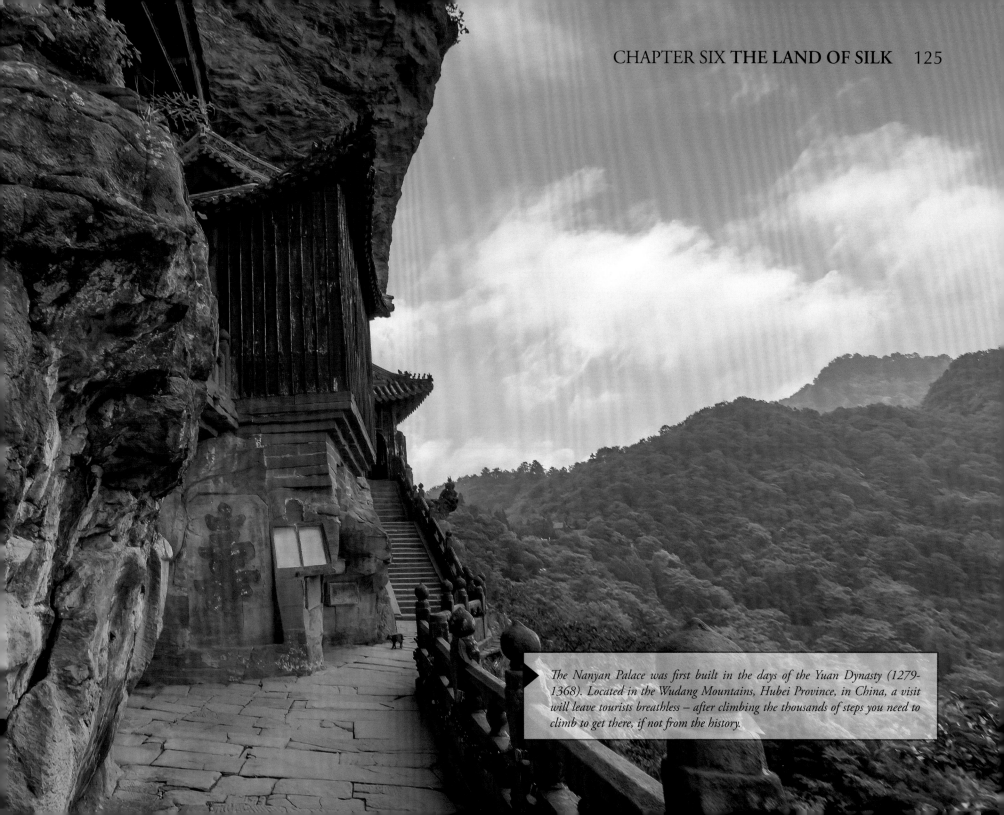

The Nanyan Palace was first built in the days of the Yuan Dynasty (1279-1368). Located in the Wudang Mountains, Hubei Province, in China, a visit will leave tourists breathless – after climbing the thousands of steps you need to climb to get there, if not from the history.

surrounded by mountains that allow only two roads to the west and two to the south. Less than a century later, the Silk Road would follow one of these western roads.

Another reason Liu Bang moved his capital to Chang'an is that it allowed him to watch over the great mausoleum of Emperor Qin Shi Huan, who united the Chinese states in 221 B.C. Located near the Qin capital of Xianyang, several kilometres downstream from Chang'an, his mausoleum contains the Terracotta Army discovered in 1974 by a group of farmers digging a well. Although most of these figures are still underground, it's estimated that there are a total of 8,000 soldiers, 130 chariots with 520 horses, and 150 cavalry horses.

Chang'an served at various times as capital of ten different dynasties, and even when the capital was moved elsewhere it remained the eastern terminus of the Silk Road. From Chang'an imported goods were distributed throughout the empire, while Chinese goods were brought to the city for export. It was a large, bustling, cosmopolitan metropolis with people from throughout Eurasia representing a myriad of cultures and religions. According to an official census in the year 742, when the city was at its height, almost two million people lived in Chang'an and the smaller cities around it. Modern estimates put the population within the city walls at 800,000 to 1,000,000 during much of the eighth century A.D., making it the largest city in the world.

Leaving the west gate of Chang'an travellers passed through the wide, fertile Wu valley, where Marco Polo saw "fine plains planted with mulberries," the trees that produce the leaves that form the only diet of the silkworms. The route through the valley, part of the Chinese Imperial Highway that crisscrossed the empire, was so well paved that wheeled carts and chariots could travel it. Chinese officials collected taxes from merchants and food and shelter was readily available.

The Yellow River at dusk in Lanzhou, China. The city, once called the "Golden City", due to the precious metal found there, was a significant fortress for over 1,400 years leading to great prosperity as a key Silk Road city.

After some 400 km, the road crossed to the upper valley of the Yellow River, and continued to the site of modern Lanzhou, 700 km from Chang'an at the entry to the Hexi Corridor. From Lanzhou, eastbound goods could be floated downriver on rafts made of inflated animal hides. Due to its strategic location, the city has been a major communications centre since the beginning of the Silk Road and is today the major railway junction for northwest China.

The Hexi Corridor

A long narrow strip more than 1,000 km long and 15-200 km wide, the Hexi Corridor is bounded by the Qilian Mountains on the south and the Gobi Desert on the north. Numerous oases, fed by snowmelt from the mountains, make it a remarkably fertile land in spite of its harsh surroundings. The brave emissary Zhang Qian spent ten years with the Xiongnu in the Hexi Corridor, and driving the nomads out of the area was the key to opening up the Silk Road to the West. The corridor was so important that the Han Dynasty extended the Great Wall through its entire length.

Ganzhou (modern Zhangye) occupied a strategic location in the centre of the corridor. Marco Polo, who spent a year in the city, described the people as "Idolators, Saracens, and Christians" referring to Buddhist, Moslems, and Nestorians. The latter, had "three very fine churches," testimony to the mark that Christianity made on China during the Silk Road period. He also noted "an enormous number of idols, both small and great." One of the great idols was a reclining Buddha, 34.5 metres long, in the Giant Buddha Temple completed in 1098. According to legend, the temple is the birthplace of Kublai Khan.

Beyond Ganzhou is the Jiayuguan Pass, which marked the transition from China into the deserts of the Western Regions. During the early years of the Ming Dynasty (1368-1644), the Great Wall was rebuilt as far as Jiayuguan, and today an impressive fortress and two looming gates still stand as they did when a steady stream of travellers from the west waited for permission to enter China—while travellers from the east ventured fearfully into the deserts. The Han Dynasty had extended their wall much further west, but the most impressive remaining sections of the Great Wall all date to the Ming Dynasty.

Dunhuang and the Taklamakan Desert

Towards the western end of the Hexi Corridor, the Silk Road split in two at Anxi, with one route heading to north of the Tien Shan Mountains toward the steppe, while another route continued onto Dunhuang, the westernmost military outpost of the Han Empire. After the Emperor Wu drove out the Xiongnu in 121 B.C., the Great Wall was extended just beyond Dunhuang to Lop Nur, a now-dry, landlocked lake at the eastern end of the Taklamakan. Desert. Dunhuang was called the "City of Sands" after the giant, drifting dunes just outside of the city that travellers would now face in their westward journey.

To the southeast of Dunhuang are the world-famous Mogao Caves, called by early twentieth century missionary-explorer Mildred Cable "an art gallery in the desert." Buddhist monks began work on the caves in A.D. 366, and for the next thousand years almost 500 caves and grottoes were carved out of the sandstone cliffs and decorated with more than 45,000 square metres of murals and 2,000 painted stucco statues. These caves and grottoes offered Silk Road travellers a place to pray for success and safety on their journey; wealthy merchants who paid monks for the artwork hoped their offering would grant them success and safety in return.

Although most of the art reflects Buddhist themes, there are also historic scenes such as the journey of Zhang Qian to the West. The Tang Dynasty paintings of Mogao are considered among the heights of Buddhist art,

The stunning Flaming Mountains, in the Xinjiang region of China, provides a notable landmark near the ancient Silk Road city of Gaochang, once a busy trading centre until it was destroyed in the fourteenth century.

▶ *The Crescent Lake (Yueyaquan in Chinese) is a desert-defying oasis six kilometres south of the Silk Road city of Dunhuang. For over 2,000 years this freshwater spring has enabled weary travellers a much needed pitstop on the Silk Road.*

with vibrant colours still preserved by the dry climate. In the early 1900s, a Buddhist abbot discovered some 50,000 manuscripts sealed in a chamber, where they were hidden during the eleventh century A.D. to protect them from invasion by the Tangut, a Mongolian people who established an empire in the area. Among the manuscripts was a printed scroll of the Diamond Sutra dating to 868, one of the oldest printed books in the world.

Dunhuang was a major crossroads, where the Silk Road met the north-south route from India and Tibet into Mongolia and Siberia. Chinese merchants typically only travelled as far as Dunhuang or Loulan, another crossroads city further west. From these cities, other traders—Sogdians, Indians, Kushans, Persians, Arabs, Uyghurs, or Mongols—had to choose their route around the brutal Taklamakan Desert. The southern route was the driest and most difficult, because the oasis cities were further apart, but from the opening of the Road to the sixth century A.D.—when there was more rainfall than in later periods—it was the most travelled because it posed less of a threat from bandits and nomadic tribesmen. The northern route had more water but was more exposed to attacks.

Each road led through a fortified mountain pass protected by a gate in the Great Wall. About 80 km north-west of Dunhuang was the Yumenguang (Jade Gate) Pass, named because of the large quantities of jade transported through the pass even before the wall was built. About 75 km to the south-west of Dunhuang was the Yanguan (South Gate) Pass. As portals to the dangers of the desert, both of these passes were celebrated by poets of the Tang Dynasty. Of the Jade Gate, Wang Zhihuan wrote, "Beyond the Yumenguan Pass the breath of Spring has never crossed." Wang Wei wrote of the South Gate, "Oh, my friend, I sincerely entreat you to have another cup of wine; you will see no more friends west out of the Yangguan Pass."

The Taklamakan Desert that inspired these verses is one of the most desolate places on earth—a thousand kilometres long, 400 kilometres wide, composed almost entirely of sand with very little vegetation. Unlike deserts in Central Asia and the Middle East, where nomads and their livestock could live, the Taklamakan was and still is virtually uninhabitable, with life only possible in the oases that line its edges. Although legend has it that the name "Taklamakan" means "if you go in you will never come out," it is more likely a Uyghur version of Arabic words meaning a place to leave alone or abandon.

Huge, windblown, reddish-golden dunes, some as high as 100 metres, spread across the desert landscape. It was infamous for mirages and strange sounds that many Silk Road travellers believed to be demons. Caravans often travelled at night to avoid the searing heat of the day, and the strange sounds were deemed especially dangerous in the darkness. According to Marco Polo, travellers that lagged behind at night "will hear spirits talking, and will suppose them to be his comrades. Sometimes the spirits will call him by name and thus shall a traveller ofttimes be led astray so that he never finds his party."

The Southern Desert Route

From around 200 B.C. to A.D. 1000, the first half of the southern desert route was controlled by the kingdom of Shanshan (originally called Loulan), which the Chinese first conquered in 77 B.C. during their campaign of western expansion. Today, several of the once-great cities along this stretch of road—Miran, Endere, and Niya—are abandoned ruins among the windswept sands. Other caravan stops have survived near modern cities: Cherchen (modern Qiemo) and Yuan (Ruoqian), once the Shanshan capital. When Marco Polo visited this area he noted that when an army attacked, the people would flee with their livestock "into the sandy wastes; and knowing the spots where water is to be had, they are able to live there, and to keep their cattle alive, whilst it is impossible to find them; for the wind immediately blows the sand over their track."

Beyond Shanshan was the Buddhist kingdom of Khotan and its ancient capital of the same name (modern Hotan or Hetian). Long before the Silk Road, Khotan was the source of the precious jade that the Yuezhi supplied to the Chinese. Located on a bountiful oasis watered by the Khotan River, it became the first area outside of ancient China to grow mulberry trees and produce silk. According to a widespread legend, a Chinese princess sent to marry the King of Khotan in the mid-fifth century A.D. smuggled forbidden silkworm eggs and mulberry seeds out of China in her hair. A century later, Nestorian monks from Khotan carried seeds and eggs to Constantinople. Today, modern Hotan is still famous for jade and silk as well as beautiful wool carpets.

West of Khotan was the kingdom and city of Yarkand (modern Shache), a strategic intersection of several trade routes. From the city, a traveller could head westward across the Pamir Mountains and continue through modern Pakistan and Afghanistan to the Silk Road city of Balkh. Another route led south into India. The most travelled route, however, continued to the north-west around the edge of the desert to Kashgar, one of the great crossroads cities of Asia.

The Northern Desert Route

In the early centuries of the Silk Road, merchants would often continue west from Dunhuang to the city of Loulan on the shore of Lop Nor, a shallow, marshy lake fed by the Tarim River. When the first Chinese emissary to the West, Zhang Qian, passed through Loulan in 126 B.C., he counted 14,000 people living within the city walls—an impressive population considering the Chinese had not yet expanded into the Tarim Basin. At that time Loulan was the capital of the independent Loulan Kingdom (renamed Shanshan by the Chinese) that dominated the eastern Taklamakan. Like Dunhuang, Loulan became a terminus for Chinese merchants to trade their goods with western middlemen, who could follow the route north of the desert, which passed through the city, or take a longer road to the south and pick up the southern route.

Around A.D. 330, however, the waters of Lop Nor moved southward as the Tarim River shifted its course. By the sixth century A.D, Loulan was abandoned and gradually disappeared into the desert until it was rediscovered in 1899 by Swedish archaeologist Sven Hedin. Extraordinarily well-preserved mummies dating as early as 3,800 B.C., some with Caucasian features, have been discovered in the Loulan area. Modern irrigation has, however, left Lop Nor as a salt encrusted dry lakebed, where the Chinese have instead tested atomic weapons.

The abandonment of Loulan in the sixth century A.D. corresponded with substantial climate change that made the Tarim Basin even drier, and it remains one of the driest and hottest places on earth. The southern route, which had less water than the north, was affected most severely, and the northern route became the primary road. With the loss of Loulan's water resource, merchants who wanted to travel this road had to detour further north through the oasis cities of Hami and Turpan. At the base of a mountain pass to the northern steppes, Turpan was not only an important city for its plentiful water and abundant agriculture, but also as a route of attack for nomadic tribes from the north and—in more peaceful times—a jumping off point for the northern steppe route of the Silk Road toward Kazakhstan. The knowledge of making grape wine, which travelled east from the Fergana Valley, was developed in Turpan before passing on to China; modern Turpan remains a major wine-producing region.

▶ *A highway snakes through the verdant mountains in Xinjiang, China. Remote from the ocean, and surrounded by high mountains, the Tien Shan mountain range separates the dry south from the less arid north, leaving the northern slopes more lush.*

Whether the westbound traveller went through Loulan or Turpan, the northern desert route led to the oasis city-states of Korla, Kucha and Aksu. Located near the centre of the route, Kucha was the largest kingdom of the Chinese Western Regions. At its height during the Tang Dynasty, the rich Silk Road trade supported Buddhist monasteries housing some 5,000 monks. The Kizil Thousand Buddhas Caves—about 75 km northwest of the city—are decorated with fine frescoes in the Gandharan style, a mixture of Indian and Greek influences carried along the Silk Road. Kuchan music, particularly the lute, was very influential on Chinese music, yet another gift passed along the Road.

Kashgar

Located at the western end of the Taklamakan Desert, surrounded on three sides by towering snow-capped mountains, Kashgar (modern-day Kashi) was perhaps the greatest crossroads of the Silk Road. At Kashgar the northern and southern routes around the Taklamakan Desert came together and met three major routes over the mountains to and from the West. Of the many great cities on the Silk Road, Kashgar was the nexus, the site where east, west, north, and south truly met.

The route leading north out of Kashgar crossed the Tien Shan through the Torugart Pass into modern Kyrgyzstan—continuing north to Lake Issuk Kul and the many Silk Road cities along the Kyrgyz-Kazakh border. The westward route crossed the Pamirs through the Irkeshtam Pass into Tajikistan and the modern Pamir Highway. From there, merchants could head north into the Fergana Valley, continue west towards Samarkand and Bukhara, or follow the snaking south-westerly route of the modern highway to Balkh.

To the south, the route followed the modern Karakoram Highway, which connects Kashgar to Islamabad, the capital of Pakistan. This route leads into the Karakorum Mountains past Lake Karakol to Tashkurgan and the

A narrow side street in one of Beijing's last remaining traditional hutong district.

Khunjerab Pass, which at 4,693 metres is one of the highest paved passes in the world. During Silk Road times, Tashkurgan was an important crossroads where travellers could take an old, well-travelled route to Balkh through the Wakhan Corridor of Afghanistan or continue south to the Indus River Valley. Tashkurgan means "stone city" in the local Tajik language, a reference to a sixth century stone fort just north of the town. A dirt road running alongside the fort is said to have arisen from the original Silk Road.

As the most western city in the Tarim Basin, the history of Kashgar is connected to Central Asia as much as it is to the history of China. During the second century A.D., it had close relations with the Buddhist Empire of Kush and may have been the first Buddhist kingdom in the Tarim Basin. Beginning in the late tenth century A.D., Kashgar became a capital of the Karakhanid Empire established by Turkic Uyghurs who had converted to Islam. The Karakhanid realm stretched into Central Asia as far as Bukhara—an indication of how closely the Silk Road connected Kashgar to the West. During the twelfth century A.D., the Karakhanids were driven out by another Turkic people called the Kara-Khitai, who favoured Buddhism and Nestorian Christianity, and forbade the practice of Islam. When the Mongols conquered Kashgar in 1219, the Uyghurs greeted them as liberators who allowed them to return to their faith.

Today, with a population of more than 350,000, Kashgar is one of the largest cities of Xinjiang Province. According to the 2003 census, 31 nationalities reside in the city. Yet more than 70% are ethnic Uyghurs, and it is China's most Muslim city, with minarets dotting the skyline and a remarkable total of 162 mosques in the Kashgar area. The fifteenth century Idkah Mosque regularly hosts almost 10,000 worshippers for Friday services and can hold as many as 20,000.

A traditional side street in modern Xi'an, China. During the days of the Silk Road the city was known as Chang'an.

Every Sunday, Kashgar is home to the Yekshenba Bazaar, a great trading frenzy that has been called the greatest market in the world. It offers a dizzying array of products from silk, figs, and raw sheepskin to modern electronics and ironmongery, amongst traditional handcrafts and souvenirs. Uyghur men have their heads shaved with lethally sharp razors, women shop for brightly coloured scarves, and acrobats and magicians entertain. A little further out of town horses, donkeys, camels, and sheep are for sale, and the air is filled with the spicy scent of mutton kebabs and fresh *nan*, a savoury flatbread found throughout Central Asia. It is said that some 100,000 people come each week from the surrounding area, including neighbouring countries, to join the citizens of Kashgar in this ritual of ancient trade. Few westerners can be found in this sea of Uyghurs and other Asians trading and haggling as they have done for two millennia. However, for those who do find their way to the Kashgar bazaar, it is easy to imagine that the years have faded away and they are among the legendary caravans and merchants of the ancient Silk Road.

Beginning or End?

Few have travelled the entire length of the Silk Road. To do so would have required great endurance, wealth and courage, likely without commensurate reward, even for the faithful. However, many have travelled along parts of this ancient trading route, often without realising the depth of the history upon which they walked nor the significance of their existence upon it. Tracing the lines of the major and minor routes attributed to the Silk Road provides endless fascination as your finger passes famous cities, some long disappeared, and crosses some of nature's highest, harshest and driest terrain. Although the Silk Road never started or ended in any one place, its history has endured across Eurasia, surviving both time and technology, ever re-inventing itself and returning to the

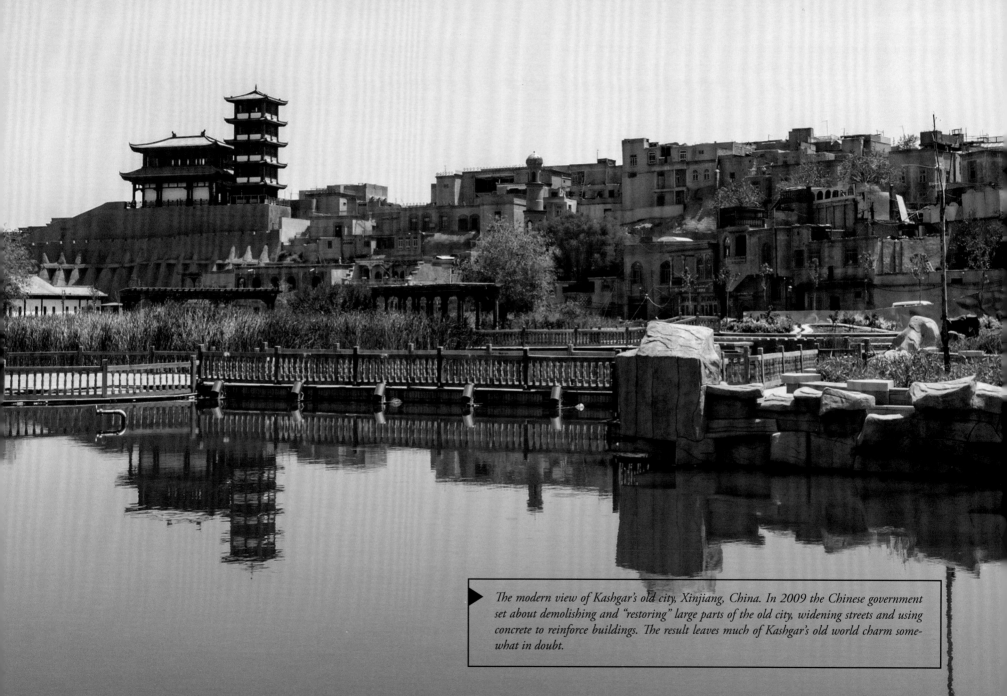

The modern view of Kashgar's old city, Xinjiang, China. In 2009 the Chinese government set about demolishing and "restoring" large parts of the old city, widening streets and using concrete to reinforce buildings. The result leaves much of Kashgar's old world charm somewhat in doubt.

forefront of our minds even in today's world. The wonderful people of the Silk Road today remain as committed to their past as to their future. As the geopolitical importance of the Silk Road emerges once again in trade and commerce between nations, so too will another chapter be written. For now, though, we must live in the present and take our chance to remember and respect everything that this great route and its people has given to modern society and will, no doubt, continue to provide for generations to come. Perhaps its greatest chapter is yet to be written.

Left & Right: From Chinese dumplings to Italian Tortellini, there are many remarkable similarities in the food styles from both east and west visible in today's cuisine, largely thanks to the Silk Road.

A serene morning meeting between traders on a river tributary to the Yangtze river, China. Rivers are not often mentioned in the Silk Road story, but they too played their part in trade.

TIMELINE OF KEY SILK ROAD HISTORICAL EVENTS

Çatalhöyük excavations (in Turkey) suggest it is the world's first city	6500	5700	B.C.
First agricultural cultures are believed to have existed in Meso-potamia and Egypt	6000	5500	B.C.
Sericulture (production of silk) discovered	2700		B.C.
Art of Metallurgy flourishes	2500	2000	B.C.
Bactrian camel domesticated	2500		B.C.
Birth of Zoroaster, who founded Zoroastrianism	c. 2300		B.C.
Birth of Judaism	1812		B.C.
Indo-European invaders (Hittites) use horse-drawn chariots to cross the Caucasus and invade Anatolia, ruling for centuries	1800	1160	B.C. B.C.
Greek invasion of Troy	1190		B.C.
Rome is founded	753		B.C.
Nomadic Scythians rule the eastern Central Asian steppe	750		B.C.
Byzantium founded as Greek colony	667		B.C.
Medes and Babylonians form an alliance to defeat the Assyrians and extend trading relations	606		B.C.
Reign of Cyrus the Great	c. 600	530	B.C.
Steppe nomads perfect the art of horse riding	600		B.C.
Birth of Buddhism thanks to the life of Siddharta Gautama Buddha who disseminated his teachings	563	483	B.C.
First Persian Empire of Cyrus the Great (Achaemenid Empire)	550	330	B.C.
Life of Confucius in China - His students form Confucianism	522	483	B.C.
Reign of Darius the Great who brought political structure and military security to the Persian Empire and Silk Road trade	522	486	B.C. B.C.
Royal Road in existence bringing trade between Persia and Ana-tolia	5th Cent.		B.C.
Reign of Alexander the Great	356	323	B.C.

Seleucid Empire	312	63	B.C.
Parthian Empire - return Persian rule after Greeks defeated	247	224	B.C./A.D.
Qin Dynasty - the First imperial dynasty of a united China	221	206	B.C.
Han Dynasty	206	220	B.C./A.D.
Sogdian Empire - probably the greatest traders on the Silk Road buffering the Persian Empire and the nomadic tribes of the Steppe	2nd Cent.	10th Cent.	B.C./A.D.
Chang'an established as Chinese capital during Han Dynasty	206		B.C.
Zhang Qian visits Central Asian territories as a Chinese envoy	138		B.C.
Yuezhi confederacy	128	450	B.C./A.D.
Emperor Wu drives Xiongnu out of Hexi Corridor and extends the Great Wall to provide safety to merchant travellers	121		B.C.
Chinese delegation sent to Persia and Silk Road fully opens	106		B.C.
Rome first becomes aware of silk	53		B.C.
Birth of Jesus Christ and Christianity (estimated)	6	4	B.C.
St Peter creates first Christian church in a cave in Antioch	1st Cent.		A.D.
Kushan Empire - disseminates Buddhism along the Silk Road	30	375	A.D.
China regains western frontier control opening trade all the way to Rome	End of 1st Cent.		A.D.
The first Roman envoy is sent to China (by sea) by Roman em-peror Marcus Aurelius	166		A.D.
Sassanid Empire	224	651	A.D.
Emperor Constantine renames Byzantium to Constantinople	330		A.D.
Fall of Western Roman Empire	476		A.D.
Secret of Silk production arrives in Europe	Early 6th Cent.		A.D.
Hagia Sophia completed in Constantinople	537		A.D.
Birth of prophet Mohammed and Islam	571		A.D.
First Islamic ambassadors arrive in China	618	620	A.D.
Tang Dynasty	619	907	A.D.

Event			
Nestorian Christians arrive in China's capital of Chang'an (modern-day Xi'an), documenting Christianity's first known contact with China	635		A.D.
Islamic Caliphates rule Persian territories	636	809	A.D.
City of Merv acts as a focal point for Umayyad Caliphate territorial and trade expansion	748	1258	A.D.
Battle of Talas - only direct military conflict between Chinese and Arab armies	751		A.D.
Venice established as a city state	800		A.D.
Samanid Dynasty	812	999	A.D.
Kharakhanid Empire - helped spread Islam across the Silk Road	840	1212	A.D.
Bukhara becomes the capital of the Samanid Dynasty and the intellectual heart of the Islamic world until destroyed by the Mongols	892	1220	A.D.
Song Dynasty - further spreads Islam in China	960	1279	A.D.
Seljuk Empire - leads the development of trade by building protected caravanserais for merchants along the Silk Road	1037	1194	A.D.
Great Schism dividing Greek and Latin churches	1054		A.D.
Reign of Malik-Shah who makes Esfahan his capital further promoting Silk Road trade south towards Mecca	1072	1092	A.D.
First Crusade	1095	1099	A.D.
Jerusalem falls to the First Crusade	1098		A.D.
Jin Dynasty	1115	1234	A.D.
Second Crusade	1147	1149	A.D.
Rule of Genghis Khan	1162	1227	A.D.
Third Crusade	1189	1192	A.D.
Fourth Crusade	1202	1204	A.D.
Mongol Empire	1206	1687	A.D.
Mongol warriors attack eastern Persian cities razing them to the ground	1220		A.D.
Marco Polo's life. He leaves Venice to travel east in 1271.	1254	1324	A.D.

Second wave of Mongol destruction ravages Northern Persia and captures Baghdad	1256	1258	A.D.
Ottoman Empire	1299	1923	A.D.
Rule of Amir Timur (Tamerlane)	1336	1405	A.D.
Samarkand is made the capital of Tamerlane's empire	1370		A.D.
Constantinople defeated by the Ottomans	1453		A.D.
Vasco da Gama makes successful sea crossing to India	1498		A.D.
Safavid Dynasty - attempt to restore the former glories of the Silk Road but ultimately fail	1501	1736	A.D.
Era of the Great Game between Imperial Russia and British India	1830	1895	A.D.
German geographer Ferdinand von Richthofen coins the term "Silk Road" to describe the overland routes			A.D.
between East Asia and civilizations to the west.	1877		A.D.
Explorers Sven Hedin, Aurel Stein and Albert Von Le Coq explore and bring back Silk Road treasures from			A.D.
the East	1890	1930	A.D.
Founding of the Turkish Republic by Mustafa Kemal Ataturk denotes the end of the Ottoman Empire	1923		A.D.
Uzbek and Turkmen Soviet Socialist Republics formed	1925		A.D.
Tajik Soviet Socialist Republic formed	1929		A.D.
Kyrgyz and Kazakh Soviet Socialist Republic formed	1936		A.D.
Dissolution of the Soviet Union	1990	1991	A.D.
Chinese President Xi Jinping announces the "Belt and Road Initiative"	2009	Est. 2049	A.D.

SELECTED BIBLIOGRAPHY & FURTHER READING

The following publications are suggested for further reading:

Baumer, Christoph *The History of Central Asia Volume 2* (LB Taurus 2014)
Beckwith, Christopher *Empires of the Silk Road* (Princeton University Press 2009)
Bonavia, Judy *The Silk Road: Xi'an to Kashgar* (Odyssey 2008)
Foltz, Richard *Religions of the Silk Road* (Griffin Trade Paperback 2000)
Frankopan, Peter *The Silk Roads: A New History of the World* (Vintage 2017)
Golden, Peter *Central Asia in World History* (Oxford University Press 2011)
Hedin, Sven *Through Asia* (General Books LLC 2009)
Hopkirk, Peter *Foreign Devils on the Silk Road* (Oxford University Press 1986)
Liu, Xinru *The Silk Road in World History* (Oxford University Press 2010)
Omrani, Bijan *Asia Overland* (Odyssey 2010)
Rowan, Nick *Friendly Steppes: A Silk Road Journey* (Hertfordshire Press 2012)
Stein, Aurel *Ruins of Desert Cathay* (first published 1907, Dover Publications 1987)
Tucker, Jonathan *The Silk Road. Art and History* (Philip Wilson Publishers 2003)
Whitfield, Susan *Life Along the Silk Road* (University of California Press 2001)
Wood, Frances *The Silk Road* (The Folio Society, London 2002)

ALSO BY NICK ROWAN:

Friendly Steppes: A Silk Road Journey
(Hertfordshire Press 2012)

Available in Hardback,
Paperback and Kindle
www.hertforshirepress.com

Friendly Steppes: A Silk Road Journey chronicles an extraordinary adventure that led intrepid traveller Nick Rowan to some of the world's most incredible and hidden places: from Venice through Eastern Europe, still recovering from brutal warfare; on to Turkey, the gateway to Asia, and much-misunderstood Iran; across the exotic steppes of Central Asia, emerging from Soviet domination; and finally, into a rapidly developing yet still mysterious China. Intertwined with the majesty of 2000 years of Silk Road history, Friendly Steppes recounts not only the author's travels but the remarkable impact that this trade route has had on modern culture.

Containing colourful stories and characters, wrapped in the local myths and legends told by the people who live along the route today, this is both an entertaining travelogue and inspiring introduction to a part of the world that has largely remained hidden from Western eyes for hundreds of years, but is now on the verge of retaking its central role on the international stage.

SPECIAL MENTION

Many people have contributed to this book either through sponsorship, providing wonderful photography, helping with the marketing and administration or bringing the logistics together. The publishing team and author are indebted to their support. A special mention goes to:

Sponsors:
Annunziata Rees-Mogg
Ant Rowan
Bella Bardswell
Carol Michaelson
Ian Mok
Iskakova Ralina
Marlene Hofer
Marley Burns
Mike Muller
Peter Broad
Ralina Iskakova
Sandy Shaw
Shahsanem Murray
Susannah Graham-Campbell
Zaher Yaqubie
& 12 Anonymous

Photographers:
Feruz Rustamov
Mukhhiddin A Lee
Dovlet Madadov
Eduard Kamenskih
James Stronsky
Zeinulla Kakimzhanov
Nina V. Belomestnova
Pavel Svoboda
Dan Lundberg
Mohamad Babayan
Hasan Almasi
Steven Su
Annie Spratt
Amit Jain
Frederica Diamanta
Till Kottmann
& others

Design: Alexandra Rey

Map: Thomas Bachrach

Author's Photo: Xander Casey

Editing & Additional Research:
Paul Robert Walker

Project Management:
Angelina Krasnogir

Publisher:
Marat (Mark)Akhmedjanov

Logistics:
Timur Akhmedjanov
Victorya Malyushitskaya